Neal Starkman

IDEAS THAT COOK

Activities for Asset Builders

in School Communities

Search INSTITUTE · Practical research benefiting children and youth

Ideas That Cook: Activities for Asset Builders in School Communities
Neal Starkman
Copyright © 2001 by Search Institute

At the time of this book's publication, all facts and figures cited are the most current available; all telephone numbers, addresses, and Web site URLs are accurate and active; all publications, organizations, Web sites, and other resources exist as described in this book; and all efforts have been made to verify them. The author and Search Institute make no warranty or guarantee concerning the information and materials given out by organizations or content found at Web sites, and we are not responsible for any changes that occur after this book's publication. If you find an error or believe that a resource listed here is not as described, please contact Client Services at Search Institute. Parents, teachers, and other adults: We strongly urge you to monitor children's use of the Internet.

10   9   8   7   6   5   4   3   2

Search Institute
615 1st Avenue Northeast, Suite 125
Minneapolis, MN 55413
612-376-8955
800-888-7828
www.search-institute.org

ISBN: 1-57482-729-4

Credits
Editor: Kathryn (Kay) L. Hong
Copy editor: Mary Byers
Design: Diane Gleba Hall
Production manager: Rebecca Manfredini

Library of Congress Cataloging-in-Publication Data
Starkman, Neal.
    Ideas that cook : activities for asset builders in school communities /
    Neal Starkman.
        p. cm.
    ISBN 1-57482-729-4 (pbk. : alk. paper)
    1. Activity programs in education. 2. Educational psychology. I. Search
    Institute (Minneapolis, Minn.) II. Title.

LB1027.25.S73 2001
371.3—dc21   2001002768

About Search Institute

Search Institute is an independent, nonprofit, nonsectarian organization whose mission is to advance the well-being of children and youth by generating knowledge and promoting its application. The institute collaborates with others to promote long-term organizational and cultural change that supports its mission.

Search Institute's Healthy Communities • Healthy Youth (HC • HY) initiative seeks to motivate and equip individuals, organizations, and their leaders to join together in nurturing competent, caring, and responsible children and adolescents. Major support for this initiative is provided by Thrivent Financial for Lutherans. Lutheran Brotherhood, now Thrivent Financial for Lutherans, is the founding national sponsor for Healthy Communities • Healthy Youth.

About This Resource

Generous support for the development of this resource was provided by Jostens Inc., Minneapolis, Minnesota, through its Jostens Our Town Foundation.

On the Cover

An aerial view of a large-scale artwork created with donated used clothing at Gibson Elementary School, Henderson, Nevada. (See The Great Ephemeral Art Project recipe.)

Contents

Place Settings
Growing up Healthy on a Diet of Developmental Assets

Why This Book Was Written

Too often we hear about all the "trouble with kids." Too often we hear about the need to "fix" young people, to "solve their problems," to prevent them from becoming even more of a burden on society than they apparently already are. Some American adults look upon the average young person as a sculptor might look upon a slab of granite: an unformed mass, ready to be shaped into a productive human being, but with jagged projections—drug use, violence, irresponsibility, rebelliousness—that have to be chiseled off before the person is ready to join society.

In this book, you're going to look at young people a little differently. Think of preparing a sumptuous meal: You assemble nutritious ingredients; you combine them in certain ways to bring out the most flavorful attributes; and you patiently wait until the appropriate chemical and physical reactions take place and provide you with what you knew was worth all the work, namely, a wonderful, healthy, delicious meal. All the components of this meal were there to begin with; as the cook, you had to take the right actions and provide the right environment for their potential to be realized.

Providing the "right" environment in which young people can flourish has occupied educators, parents, and philosophers for untold years. But one advantage of being at the end of those untold years is that we now have some models to look at. Some things, in fact, *have* worked. We're pretty sure, for example, that a loving environment works better than a hostile one, that respect works better than contempt, that education works better than ignorance. We do have some starting points.

And those starting points are the springboards for the activities in this book. These activities come from all over the country and from different socioeconomic and geographical environments. They work, in part, because the adults involved in them are dedicated to promoting the strengths of young people, and also because the situation was right for this kind of activity. But they work, too, because the activities are just plain good ideas.

This book is dedicated to the simple proposition that good ideas implemented by competent, caring, and responsible people will work.

The Importance of Developmental Assets

This is a book of activities that build developmental assets, but what are developmental assets? Think of them as building blocks—relationships, experiences, values, attitudes, and attributes—that all children and youth need for success. Search Institute has identified 40 of these building blocks as being associated with young people's success in school—academic success, social success, and the avoidance of high-risk behaviors such as chemical use, violence, and early sexual activity. You can find a list of these assets at the end of this book, but you probably know most of them already. Here are a few:

1. **Family support**—Family life provides high levels of love and support.
8. **Youth as resources**—Young people are given useful roles in the community.
15. **Positive peer influence**—Young people's best friends model responsible behaviors.
17. **Creative activities**—Young people spend three or more hours per week in lessons or practice in music, theater, or other arts.
21. **Achievement motivation**—Young people are motivated to do well in school.
26. **Caring**—Young people place high value on helping other people.
32. **Planning and decision making**—Young people know how to plan ahead and make choices.
40. **Positive view of personal future**—Young people are optimistic about their personal future.

So far, this seems like common sense, right? Search Institute, however, has conducted research on over a million students in grades 6–12 to measure the extent to which they have the 40 developmental assets, and the results are not as rosy as you might hope. Sixth-grade students report having an average of 21.5 assets, barely more than half. But that's good, considering what happens over the next six years: 8th-grade students report having an average of 17.8 assets, 10th-grade students an average of 16.9 assets, and 12th-grade students an average of 17.2 assets.

These numbers become significant when you look at the relationship between levels of assets and high-risk behaviors. For example, 53 percent of young people with 0–10 assets report high alcohol use, compared to just 3 percent of young people with 31–40 assets. Similar results obtain with desirable behaviors: 7 percent of young people with 0–10 assets report they get mostly A's on their report cards, compared to 53 percent of young people with 31–40 assets.[1] So the data are clear: More assets mean more success and less trouble.

It's also clear where young people can receive—or not receive—these assets: school, home, and the community. The focus in this book is the school. Why?

- School is where young people spend most of their waking hours;
- School is where organized activities take place, where relationships can grow, where young people are socialized;
- School is where students are surrounded by adults, many of whom have deliberately chosen careers in which they can help young people thrive; and
- School is where students are supposed to learn, where they're supposed to be safe and healthy, and where they're supposed to become productive, responsible citizens—as we've seen, all characteristics that are correlated with developmental assets.

The activities in this book thus center on the school. Some of them can be facilitated only in a school setting; some are based in a school but can extend to other communities. There are a few activities in this book that aren't set in a school at all, but can be initiated or coordinated by schools. And virtually all the activities can be incorporated into a school's core curriculum—into language arts, mathematics, science, social studies, and the rest. The more you can make these activities the norm—that is, the more they can become a part of everyday school life—the stronger the asset message will be.

Let's get more specific, though, about who can build developmental assets and who can use this book. The answer is—everyone. In the school community, the list of "cooks" includes not only teachers but principals, secretaries, librarians, cafeteria workers, aides, counselors, nurses, bus drivers, coaches, and students as well. Throw in parents, siblings, other

---

[1] From P. L. Benson, P. C. Scales, N. Leffert, and E. C. Roehlkepartain, *A Fragile Foundation: The State of Developmental Assets among American Youth* (Minneapolis, MN: Search Institute, 1999).

relatives, and members of youth-serving organizations and faith communities and businesses and government and law enforcement and service clubs and media. You'll find many of those people represented in this book.

In short, if you have access to groups of young people, or if you know people who have access to groups of young people, then you can use these activities.

After the Awareness

It's one thing to personally espouse building developmental assets. It's another to spread the word about assets, so that everyone's using the same language and is appreciating the philosophy behind promoting young people's strengths. It's another thing altogether to take the specific, concrete steps to begin the actual building of the assets. There's a world of difference between recognizing that developmental assets are important and deliberately building them. *Deliberately building them*—that's the key. We are seeking ways to *deliberately* give young people useful roles, to motivate them to do well in school, and to provide them opportunities to help other people. Search Institute has identified three basic strategies for building developmental assets in school communities; these three strategies are addressed within the activities contained in this book.

1. Relationships. Building assets begins with forming and maintaining a strong, genuine, caring, mutually respectful relationship between a young person and an adult. It makes all the difference in the world to young people if they know that an adult thinks they're special, thinks they can "make it," thinks that they're a good human being. That's why you see so many activities in this book featuring "mentoring," in which teachers or counselors or nurses or secretaries or people from the community take students under their wing, check on how they're doing in school, inquire about their needs, offer support, and so on. The relationship is the basis for building the assets; the young person has someone to learn from, to lean on, and to strive for.

2. Environment. Environment is many things. For one, it's the physical surroundings. When students come to school, what do they see? Do they see dark hallways that all look alike, austere classrooms, barred windows and doors, peeling paint, and broken equipment? Or do they see brightly lit corridors festooned with plants and student artwork, classrooms brimming with the day's activities, open doors and windows, well-kept facilities, and working—if not new—equipment? The former environment gives the message, "We don't care"; the latter says, "Come on in!"

Environment is also people. What happens when students—and adults, for that matter—first enter the school building? Are they greeted by surly security guards or by a smiling principal and staff? Are they called by a "Hey, you" or by their first name? Do school staff adopt a "not my kid, not my problem" attitude or an "all kids are our kids" attitude? Think about where you work, or where you'd like to work: Which type of environment motivates *you* to do your best, enjoy yourself, and stay out of trouble?

3. Programs and practices. The third basic strategy to building assets is to implement programs and practices that give young people opportunities to thrive. Sometimes those programs and practices are already in place, and you need merely to focus them a bit more to make the asset building intentional. At other times you have to alter what's going on in order to redirect people's efforts toward asset building. A typical example is an athletic program that's characterized by humiliating students and otherwise punishing them for not meeting adult expectations of winning. There's nothing wrong with the program per se, but its personnel, philosophy, and norms need to be redirected to building young people up rather than tearing them down. At still other times, you may want to import an activity that's totally new; hence this book. These programs, practices, activities—call them what you will—can be implemented community-wide, schoolwide, and classroom-wide. They can be as complex as restructuring the school so that students form a network of councils in which they make decisions and act as a liaison between themselves and school adults (see Neighborhood Youth Councils under Main Courses) or as simple as rewarding students for acts of kindness (see Kindness Chains under Side Dishes).

It's good to recognize the value of the developmental assets framework, and it's good to publicize it. Important as those steps are, however, those are merely preparations for the journey. It's another, gigantic step to actually set forth on that journey, to go about the business of building assets for and *with* young people. This book is about creative ways to take that journey.

How This Book Is Organized

There are many good reasons for approaching the activities described here as if they were recipes:

- When you read a recipe, you're assured that someone, somewhere, has successfully made this meal before. That gives you confidence that *you* can make it. In this book, I give you the name, address, and phone number of each "**chef**"—the person who has developed or who implements the activity. These chefs are the people you should contact if you want more information. They may be principals, teachers, leaders of organizations, students, or parents; they're in this book because they want to tell people about their asset-building activity.

- When you read a recipe, you can get some idea about how healthy the meal will be for the people who eat it. In this book, I identify the "**nutrients**"—the developmental assets promoted in each activity. I've listed the three most pronounced assets promoted by the activity. How the activity is implemented and what the students put into it are just two of the factors that determine which assets are addressed, but simply by doing the activity, you'll be promoting the assets. And in many cases, building the asset will depend on *how* you interact with the young people. Remember, you can always alter an activity if you want to focus on a specific asset. Add lemon juice to a recipe and you get more vitamin C; add small-group work to an activity and you get the potential for more Asset #15—Positive peer influence.

- A recipe usually tells you how many people it **serves;** you can also probably figure out the extent to which it's a recipe for adults (coq au vin) or for kids (cucumber-and-peanut-butter alien sandwiches). In this book, I tell you how many young people in which grades the activity initially served. Virtually all the activities, however, have the potential to serve many more people—adults as well as young people—than they currently do. The activities can be expanded, shifted to other arenas, and modified in any number of ways—just as a recipe for chili for four can be modified to feed an army of vegetarians. For example, many of the activities developed in a high school could be adapted to suit the developmental needs of students in a middle school or elementary school.

- A recipe tells you which **ingredients** are required so that you can decide beforehand if you're able to make it. In this book, I list what you'll need to implement the activity. The ingredients will vary depending on who is facilitating the activity, but I've listed any unusual or specific materials required. The main ingredients in all these activities are human—the individuals and organizations that put forth time, energy, and sometimes money to make these activities work.

- When you read a recipe the way my wife, Chris, does, you follow the **instructions** to the nth degree: Add half a teaspoon of walnut oil, beat the eggs for exactly two minutes, and don't you dare uncover the pot while the rice is boiling, even for a second. When you read a recipe the way I do, you take it all in, stroke your chin, and immediately begin improvising: walnut oil's too expensive, so I'll use olive oil; and I think I'll add some nutmeg to those eggs; and the cosmos won't be upset if I just peek at that rice. In this book, you can have it both ways: I've identified the steps of the activity as explicitly as possible—for the most part, sticking to the chef's recipe—but I've left plenty of leeway for you to adapt the activity to your own young people with your own resources in your own circumstances. Each recipe includes a section called "**Variations**" that suggests different ways to adapt the activity while still retaining its integrity.

- Many people I've talked to about these recipes have been most generous: They've sent photographs, memoranda, reflections, and even entire manuals describing what they've done. In truth, they've done much more than describe an activity; they've *shared an experience*. Therefore, I've included some of these "**Extra Helpings**" in order for you to get a better feel for the recipe.

So, do what works for you. Follow these recipes precisely—or experiment, substitute, and adapt. Or, start out following the recipes precisely, and *then* experiment, substitute, and adapt. Think about your resources, your young people's capabilities and needs, and the character of your school community. An alert, though: Just as you can't reliably leave the eggs out of a recipe for lemon meringue pie, and a quiche made with cream cheese instead of Swiss cheese isn't going to be nearly as successful, there are some requirements. Think about how you're adapting the activity, and be sure that it's still accomplishing what it was designed to do. If you're not sure, that's when I recommend you call the chefs.

Just as in "real" cookbooks, these recipes are divided into courses; each course is explained on its opening page. Basically, though, you can look for appetizers (start-up activities that promote assets), main courses (activities that require a bit of work and that are—or can become—a mainstay of a school), side dishes (activities that affect only a small portion of a school or community), and desserts (activities that are fairly easy to do and that everyone loves). There's nothing sacred about the divisions—and, again, implementation is everything—so do browse through the entire book. You never know what might pique your palate.

A final note about the recipes in this book: I selected them in various ways, and I could have selected thousands of others. Asset-building activities are without a doubt occurring in your community, in your schools, in your classrooms, and in your families. Some of the people involved in these activities may have no idea what a developmental asset is, at least by that name. But they know what makes a good relationship, what makes a good environment, and what makes a good program. Supporting these activities with the asset framework gives everyone a common way to speak about them; and the reason that's important is that it makes explicit what we all need to do in order to help young people grow up healthy, caring, and responsible. When you implement the activities in this book, implement them *deliberately*. Know what you're aiming for, and why; that way, you'll be sure when you reach it.

A final note about the book itself: Check out the charts at the end of the book, in the Planning Your Meals section. There you can find sample menus, and the activity "recipes" categorized by state, by assets addressed, and by area of school life. I'm hoping that these charts facilitate your use of the book but don't lead you to ignore recipes that might not be the usual ones you'd choose. Tuna casseroles are fine, but sometimes you just need to try that zucchini flan!

Companion Pieces to This Book

Search Institute has published quite a few resources that can help you build assets in your community (for a catalog, call Search Institute at 800-888-7828). Here are some resources that you might find particularly helpful when you're contemplating doing the activities in this book:

> *Great Places to Learn: How Asset-Building Schools Help Students Succeed* (1999)
> *"You Have to Live It": Building Developmental Assets in School Communities* (1999) (video)
> Handouts and Overheads from *Great Places to Learn* (2000)
> *Pass It On! Ready-to-Use Handouts for Asset Builders* (1999)
> *Developmental Assets: A Synthesis of the Scientific Research on Adolescent Development* (1999)
> *A Fragile Foundation: The State of Developmental Assets among American Youth* (1999)

Search Institute also has a Web site—www.search-institute.org.

Appetizers

APPETIZERS are activities for those just getting started. They're often fairly easy to implement, don't require a lot of preparation or materials, and provide benefits soon after implementation. Appetizers are ideal for schools, districts, or organizations that haven't yet begun to intentionally build assets; they illustrate in a modest way what can happen when people turn their attention to focusing on the positive. They're also good for people already into asset building who want to add a light touch to a "meal."

THE ALASKA GAME

In 1998, the Association of Alaska School Boards came out with *Helping Kids Succeed—Alaska Style*, a book of ideas for building assets in Alaskan communities based on the developmental assets framework. Shortly thereafter, Derek Peterson, director of child and youth advocacy on the board, began to introduce a game based on the asset framework to villages throughout the state. The game was used in community meetings as a way of getting young people and neighborhood adults to talk about assets. It was very successful: "People leave more bonded than when they came," says Peterson about the game. Today more than 1,000 copies of the game are being used virtually everywhere in Alaska; people are talking about assets, and they're building assets. Peterson observes, "The asset framework is embedded in everything we do."

Playing the game, which is also called "Helping Kids Succeed," provides opportunities for the following to be shared:

- The current perspective of young people;
- The perspective young people may have when they're an adult;
- The perspective young people have concerning their role in building assets for and with peers and young children;
- The current perspective of adults; and
- The historical perspective of adults.

What follows are generic instructions for the game (see the Association of Alaska School Boards Web site at www.aasb.org); each community can develop its own questions—according to its circumstances, population, resources, and needs—that are based on the developmental assets.

Ingredients

Cards of questions based on the asset framework
A coin to flip

Instructions

1 Develop the following cards based on the asset framework:

▶ 30 YOUTH cards, each with two questions on it, one for adults to read and the other for youth to read
  - The adult question asks adults to remember when they were teenagers and respond to the question accordingly (e.g., "When you were 16 years old, what did the concept of a 'supportive' family mean to you?").
  - The youth question asks teenagers to think about the current realities of being a teenager and respond to the question accordingly (e.g., "What is the best advice that you have ever received from your parents?").

▶ 30 ADULT cards, each with two questions on it, one for adults to read and the other for youth to read
  - The adult question asks adults to think about how they view teenagers in general and respond to the question accordingly (e.g., "What is the most helpful advice you ever gave a young person?").
  - The youth question asks teenagers to project into the future the kind of world they'll create for youth and respond to the question accordingly (e.g., "When you are 40 years old, what kind of advice will you give to young people?").

▶ 14 OPTION cards
  - For follow-up questions
  - For repeat questions
  - For passes to each player

▶ 16 WILD cards (each player in the group answers the question)

▶ 8 CHOICE cards (the group can decide either to end the game or to continue)

2 Discuss the purpose and then the general rules of the game:

▶ Players take turns answering questions—briefly and from the heart—while the rest of the group listens without responding.
▶ The ADULT cards are placed in one pile and the YOUTH cards in another pile, both near the center of the group. Each player flips a coin to determine whether to draw an ADULT card or a YOUTH card.
▶ Adults always answer the adult question on a card, and youth always answer the youth question.
▶ The player reads the card aloud and answers it, and then it's the next player's turn.

3 When the group decides to end the game, have them debrief with questions similar to the following:

▶ "What one thing did you learn about yourself from playing the game?"
▶ "If an adult, what did you learn about today's youth? If a youth, what did you learn about today's adults?"
▶ "What one thing would you like to say to all the players?"
▶ "What was the most difficult thing you had to do during the game?"

Chef

Derek Peterson, *director of child and youth advocacy,* Association of Alaska School Boards, 316 West 11th Street, Juneau, AK 99803, 907-586-1083, dpeterson@aasb.org

Nutrients

#4—Caring neighborhood, #2—Positive family communication, #36—Peaceful conflict resolution

Serves

Four to seven players at a time, preferably at least two adults and two teenagers

Variations

▶ Once you've developed the questions and adapted the play of the game, you can use it at any gathering where you want to encourage constructive communication between adults and young people; for example:
  • Students and school adults
  • Young people and community adults
  • Young people and representatives of youth-serving organizations
  • Families
▶ You can use the responses from the players as a springboard for ideas to build specific assets.

THE ASSET BANNER RUN-WALK-CRAWL

This is one of those ideas that seem to work amazingly well for many different reasons. First, it publicizes and promotes the assets. Second, it brings the community together and increases awareness of community services. Third, it provides a fun—and energizing—event for families and youth groups to participate in. Fourth, it's an opportunity for the community to show young people that they're a priority. And last, it helps to raise money for youth services. Pittsford, New York's event, by all accounts, is a tremendous success, and the coordinators plan to make it a regular occurrence.

Ingredients

Representatives from community organizations
Signs highlighting assets
Access to running route
Refreshments
Gymnastics mat
Volunteers to plan and facilitate the event

Instructions

1 In conjunction with Red Ribbon Week—a national event intended to increase community awareness of drug issues—get permission from the appropriate authorities to set up a five-kilometer route through the community; draw up maps describing it.

2 With help from students, select about 20 assets that either students report are lacking or people in the community can help build (i.e., external assets)—or both.

3 Make up signs (e.g., banners or sandwich boards) listing and describing the asset.

4 Solicit representatives from community organizations that can represent each asset to the public, for example:

▶ #1—Family support: Parent Teacher Student Association

▶ #8—Youth as resources: Pittsford Youth Services Youth Advisory Board

▶ #9—Service to others: "Food Cupboard"

▶ #10—Safety: Fire (or Police) Department Band

▶ #12—School boundaries: School Board

▶ #15—Positive peer influence: Middle School Peer Helpers

▶ #16—High expectations: Honor Society

Assign these representatives to stations—tables, booths, and so on—at places along the route, where they can dispense information.

Community members staff the Adult Role Models asset station along the course.

5 Solicit participation from merchants, service organizations, and other groups to help organize the event, direct traffic, donate money for "Asset Banner Run-Walk-Crawl" T-shirts, donate prizes for the fastest runners, and so on.

6 Publicize the event, and encourage families, students, staff, and youth groups to participate.

7 Hold a 5K run at the beginning of the event; consider charging a small entry fee.

8 After the runners take off, begin the 5K walk part of the event. Give participants a list of developmental assets so that they can check off each asset station they go by and be eligible, for example, for raffle prizes.

9 Conduct a five-foot "baby crawl" on a gymnastics mat.

10 Serve refreshments for everyone after the event.

Chef

Christine Cox, *partnership coordinator,* Pittsford Central School District, 42 West Jefferson Road, Pittsford, NY 14534, 716-218-1787, christine_cox@ pittsford.monroe.edu (working with the executive director, Pittsford Youth Services)

Nutrients

#13—Neighborhood boundaries, #4—Caring neighborhood, #7—Community values youth

Serves

200 people

Variations

▶ You can offer extra credit to students if they or their families participate; make allowances for students with special needs, for example, a Run-Walk-Wheel-Crawl.

▶ You can encourage coaches to use the 5K run as a team-conditioning event.

ASSETS FROM A HAT

The book *Building a Better Me: 40 Ways to Build Your Own Assets* (published by Lutheran Brotherhood) inspired Marlo Simpson to do this activity with her 8th-grade consumer science class. As with many activities whose purpose is to increase awareness about developmental assets, the key here is to use this as a springboard to actually help build the assets. For example, in nearby Madison Middle School, another class uses this activity to come up with asset-related activities and then also follows through with them. This particular activity would follow a general introduction to developmental assets.

Ingredients

> *Paper, colored markers, poster paper, tape, and other art supplies*
> *A hat*
> *School adults willing to be judges*
> *Permission to display posters in school hallways*

Instructions

1 Arrange the class into groups of three.

2 Write the names of the 12 assets with the lowest percentages according to Search Institute's aggregate survey data (#2—Positive family communication, #4—Caring neighborhood, #5—Caring school climate, #6—Parent involvement in schooling, #7—Community values youth, #8—Youth as resources, #14—Adult role models, #17—Creative activities, #25—Reading for pleasure, #32—Planning and decision making, #34—Cultural competence, #35—Resistance skills) on small pieces of paper and then fold the pieces in half.

3 Put the folded pieces of paper into a hat.

4 Have each group draw an asset.

5 Give each group a specific amount of time (e.g., two days) to "sell" their asset to the school by creating signs and posters and displaying them in the hallway.

6 Choose teachers to judge the signs and posters on creativity.

7 Discuss these assets with the students; focus on which assets they think are most important and which ones they think they might have or not have.

Chef

Marlo Simpson, *prevention specialist,* Adams Middle School, 1200 South McDonald Road, North Platte, NE 69101, 308-534-6029

Nutrients

#15—Positive peer influence, #24—Bonding to school, #5—Caring school climate

Serves

35 students, grade 8

Variations

▶ You can broaden the scope of the project. In addition to posters, let students create public service announcements or put on skits or use any other strategy they can think of to get their message across. You can expand the time of the project, too. It could last for a semester, for example, during which time you could help students line up outside speakers to support various messages. Finally, this could easily be a schoolwide project: Each participating class could pick several assets from a hat, or you could assign one asset category to several classes.

▶ You can let the students themselves vote on the most effective awareness campaign.

BRONCO CHOICE 2000

Many young people may feel that their community doesn't care about them because they aren't aware of what the community offers them. This activity is a way to remedy that situation. A Youth Action Team, consisting of about 300 (out of 1,800) high school students, put on Bronco Choice 2000 as a way to promote positive alternatives to using alcohol and other drugs ("Bronco" refers to the school mascot). Student assistance counselor Susan Baber got administrative permission, secured the services of the maintenance grounds crew, and called places she knew around town to have booths at the event. The event was held from 11:00 A.M. to 1:45 P.M.; students visited the booths during lunch hour, and teachers signed up to bring their students by before and after lunch hour. The local Parent Teacher Student Association made a box lunch for each person staffing a booth.

About 20 organizations participated; they included a karate center, climbers, art classes, fabric and craft stores, several recreation and park districts, and three counseling centers. Students supported the event in a variety of ways: They made a diagram of the booths and distributed them to English classes so that other students could more easily find each organization. Members of the school's Youth Action Team were assigned to each booth to take care of the community people's needs. And students also sent thank-you letters to the participating organizations. The result of Bronco Choice 2000? Students who did want alternatives to using alcohol and other drugs now had a better idea of just what some of those positive alternatives were.

Ingredients

Liaison with community agencies

Coordination within the school

A place to hold the event, along with tables, chairs, and other equipment

Lunches for participating organizations

Instructions

1 Set a date and time for the event.

2 About a month and a half before the event, call the organizations in which students might be interested and solicit their participation.

3 About a week and a half before the event, send a letter to the organizations reminding them when and where to come, and suggest ways they can present their activities.

4 Organize students, and coordinate the event within the school.

5 Provide lunch for the representatives of the organizations.

6 Allow teachers to bring their classes to the event before and after the lunch hour.

7 Have teachers assign a few students from their classes to find out about local counseling and substance abuse service resources, and then to report to their respective classes.

8 After the event, send thank-you cards to all participants.

Chef

Susan Baber, *student assistance counselor/interventionist,* Bella Vista High School, 8301 Madison Avenue, Fair Oaks, CA 95628, 916-971-5023

Nutrients

#31—Restraint, #35—Resistance skills, #37—Personal power

Serves

1,800 students, grades 9–12

Variations

▶ You can let a committee of students choose the organizations to be represented at the event; for communities with limited resources, consider choosing services within the school district that students may not know that much about.

▶ You can require that each student write a report about one of the organizations.

BUS GREETERS

This is a good idea made great by its simplicity. When Ruth Vollmer was at Valencia Elementary School, about 380 of the school's 460 students came to school on seven school buses between 8:30 and 8:45 in the morning. Vollmer chose 4th graders to greet the other students as they arrived at school—to say hi, ask them how they were doing, point the way to a classroom, and so on. The activity was an immediate success: The 4th graders felt competent because they did a job well, and they felt important because they were able to help other students—those in their own grade as well as younger students. In fact, the activity became so popular that parents wanted to rearrange their children's schedules so that they could become greeters.

Ingredients

Badges
Bus schedules

Instructions

1 Choose students who don't come to school on buses—or who come to school on the first bus—to be greeters.

2 Provide the greeters with badges and assign each of them a bus.

3 Show the greeters how to greet by name the students coming off the buses. Ask them to find out which classes the bus students are in and to make small talk; for example, ask them what they plan to do today or how they like their class.

Chef

Ruth Vollmer, *school nurse,* Bosque Farms Elementary School, P.O. Box 1300, Los Lunas, NM 87031, 505-869-2646

Nutrients

#33—Interpersonal competence, #5—Caring school climate, #24—Bonding to school

Serves

Students, grades pre-K–4

Variations

▶ This strategy—of using older students to help younger students feel more comfortable at school—is a powerful one, and you can obviously use any combination of ages in your school. You can also identify which students are responsible for which others, for example, by pairing students from different classes.

▶ You can take the strategy a step further by making the "greeters" into "guides"—designated "upper-classmates" who can be sought out by younger students for low-level information, guidance, and support.

THE DINING ROOM

There are two lunch periods in Erie Day School—one for the 120 students in preschool through grade 4 and the other for the 60 students in grades 5 through 8. What Erie Day School does for the latter lunch period is quite special. They have formal lunches, with faculty and other staff sharing both food and conversation with students. The conversation is often illuminating. At one lunch, a 5th-grade student said to the headmaster, conversationally, "I'm really proud of you. You put together a good school here." It's all very civilized, and it's a stage for modeling "grown-up" behaviors. As someone at the school said by way of description, "You're not eating, you're dining."

Ingredients

6-foot tables
Tablecloths, plates, glasses, large bowls, platters, silverware, napkins

Instructions

1 Arrange for everyone to sit at tables, each table having one faculty or other staff member and eight or nine students, two each from grades 5, 6, 7, and 8 (you can play with the numbers of students who are selected to dine with faculty, but it's probably a good idea to keep the ratio of students to teacher between 5:1 and 10:1).

2 Assign students to their table for a month and then rotate them to a different table.

3 Purchase tablecloths, plates, large bowls, silverware, napkins, etc.—perhaps from an outlet store.

4 Dine family style. Make the atmosphere as conducive to "good" behavior as possible.

Chef

Ginny Rogers, *middle school coordinator,* Erie Day School, 1372 West 6th Street, Erie, PA 16505, 814-452-4273

Nutrients

#24—Bonding to school, #3—Other adult relationships, #14—Adult role models

Serves

60 students, grades 5–8

Variations

▶ You can have a lot of fun setting up the dining situation, for example, with place cards or fancy napkin arrangements or soft background music. You don't have to spend a lot, either. You can fold paper towels in clever ways, you can play a radio station with soft music, you can use "fancy" plastic dinnerware or have art classes make ceramic plates, and so on. You can even assign the "dinner tasks"—setting the table, serving, and cleaning up—to both students and staff.

▶ You can incrementally approach this situation by beginning to make small yet progressive changes: dimming the lights in the cafeteria, arranging the seating, assigning seats, and adding tableware—gradually changing the norm from "eating" to "dining."

THE FESTIVAL OF NATIONS

Youth Day activities are part of the Walsh County Fair, in Park River, North Dakota; the fair is held every October. Last year the activities included the Festival of Nations, some of the nations being the Czech Republic, Denmark, and the Netherlands. This activity does take some coordination—that's why it helps if it's part of a larger event—but I've categorized it as an "appetizer" because it serves as a fun, nonthreatening way to introduce students to different cultures.

Ingredients

> *Representatives of different countries, along with food, clothing, literature, and other aspects of the cultures of those countries*
>
> *An auditorium*
>
> *Publicity*
>
> *High school volunteers*
>
> *Coordination of teachers' lesson plans*
>
> *"Passports" and stamps*

Instructions

1 Contact people in your community who are from countries other than the United States and who have access to accurate information and authentic illustrations of those countries' cultures.

2 Invite them to set up tables at a Festival of Nations, in which students learn about the countries by, for example, looking at native clothing, tasting native foods, and hearing the native music and languages.

3 Arrange an auditorium or other large space to accommodate all the tables on the preselected date.

4 Use the entire school community to publicize the event.

5 Ask teachers to tie the event to classroom assignments, which, for example, could consist of questions ranging from "What did all the representatives have in common?" to "What is unique about each culture?"

6 Use high school students to act as guides for younger students, perhaps one high school student for every 10 younger students.

7 Make up passports for students, and arrange to have the passports stamped with the name of the country they "visit."

8 Set up the event so that when students come in, they register, get a passport, meet their guide, and spend an ample amount of time at each table.

Chef

Ruth Jelinek, *coordinator,* Healthy Community Coalition, 115 Vivian Street, Park River, ND 58270, 701-284-4589, hcc@polarcomm.com

Nutrients

#34—Cultural competence, #22—School engagement, #33—Interpersonal competence

Serves

100 students, grades 1–12

Variations

▶ If the identities of the countries are known beforehand, you can have teachers help students learn something about the countries, including the native language, so that the students can interact more with the representatives. You can find out the home countries of your community's largest immigrant populations and start with those.

▶ You can ask students whose families are from the selected countries to meet with the representatives, help prepare the exhibits, and work at the tables.

LETTERS OF ENCOURAGEMENT

Twenty-eight years ago, Anna Johnson's employer received a letter from a customer who complimented her work; he then shared the letter at a staff meeting. The letter arrived at a time in Johnson's life when she desperately needed a boost. She never forgot that incident, and only last year put the memory into practice with her own program to give other people a similar boost. Johnson calls herself a "warrior to spread encouraging words." For the past two years, she has lined up a sponsor; purchased stamps, stationery, and envelopes; and set up shop at a table in a mall, where she offers free delivery to anyone who wants to send an encouraging letter. Last year she received $500 from her sponsor and sent 1,148 letters.

One person sent a note of encouragement to a TV talk-show host. As it happens, the host received the note on the very day that his show was canceled. He responded, and the two have kept up a correspondence. One teacher offered extra credit for her students who sent notes; the following year, the people—students and adults—who *received* the notes came to send some. A teenager sent letters to her teachers, parents, and grandparents; she said the letters to the teachers weren't intended to be bribes, but she felt that her teachers worked hard and needed a pat on the back.

"People write to everyone," says Johnson, "and it snowballs." This is another of those simple ideas made elegant by its implementation. It builds assets for the person who sends the letter and for the person who receives it.

Ingredients

Funds for postage
Mailing supplies
Access to a mall or other place visited by large numbers of people

Instructions

1 Secure sponsorship to pay for the costs of postage and mailing supplies.

2 Gain access to a mall or similar location (like the main school lobby) where you can set up your table.

3 Print copies of a form letter that offers words of encouragement.

4 Offer people the opportunity either to write a letter or to add their words to the form letter, and then to mail it at no cost.

Chef

Anna Johnson, 101 West Lincoln, Suite 201, Tullahoma, TN 37388, 931-461-9127, mentor@midtnn.net

Nutrients

#38—Self-esteem, #4—Caring neighborhood, #26—Caring

Serves

An unlimited number of people

Variations

▶ While Johnson's effort is open to anyone, you can scale down the activity to a group of students. You provide the postage and the motivation, and they write the letters. (Students unable to write—for whatever reason—can dictate letters.) They can also include photographs, drawings, and anything else they like that conforms to your postage budget. (You can even do it only within the school community and save postage.)

▶ You can make this a regular event, for example, by designating certain days as letter-writing days. You can also "infuse" it into your core language arts curriculum.

 **See EXTRA HELPINGS**

EXTRA HELPINGS for *Letters of Encouragement: (a) An invitational flyer for the event; (b) A sample form letter of encouragement; (c) A thank-you letter from a participant.*

You're Invited to Participate in
► Tullahoma's Make a Difference Day Event ◄

WHAT: *Encouraging Words Make a Difference*

WHERE: Northgate Mall, center court, Tullahoma

WHEN: Tomorrow, Saturday, October 28, from noon to 3 P.M.

HOW: Bring the names and addresses of up to five people you would like to honor or recognize with a special note. We will have the paper and envelopes. After you write and seal your letters, we'll apply a special stamp to the envelopes. If you don't want to write a full letter, use our special forms. Just sign, seal, and we'll deliver! This project will not cost you a penny. The folks at THOMPSON FORD are taking care of the postage! Your letters can go anywhere in the United States. So, write your old college buddy, a friend, teacher, political figure, movie star, parents, siblings, customers . . . This project is open to all ages. Toddlers will be provided with crayons for their "artwork."

WHY: There are so many folks who go to bed each night, hungry due to lack of food. There are even more people going to bed hungry for a kind word, or a bit of encouragement. We are offering you an opportunity to help make a difference by spreading an encouraging word!

For more information about this project, contact . . .

(a)

Dear _____,

You are very special! Your friend decided to honor you today, by taking part in the citywide "Make a Difference Day" project.

Today, hundreds of citizens from Tullahoma, TN, are mailing notes like this one, to family, friends, and other folks who deserve to be recognized. *You are appreciated!*

We hope you get a nice, warm glow because someone cared enough to send best wishes your way. If you enjoyed such a feeling, pass it on!

(b)

Anna:

I don't think words can accurately portray the spirit of caring present at the "Letters of Encouragement" event in conjunction with Make a Difference Day. I brought a few of my own greeting cards to mail out and found that once I started writing, I couldn't stop. Since the coordinators of the program provided small sheets of paper with words of encouragement, I mailed out several others that were individualized with personal messages.

My little sister was the recipient of one of these letters. She had just begun her freshman year in high school, and I had been looking for a way to talk to her about some difficult things going on in her life. On the back of the paper, I told her that I loved her, I am there for her whenever she needs me, high school years are very challenging times for her and her friends, but she is capable of being the wonderful young lady I know she is.

The day she received my letter, she told me that she almost cried when she read it. I realized that I don't tell her these things often enough. When I visited her house last week (months after the event), I noticed that same note sitting on a table in her room.

I hope everyone who participated in "Letters of Encouragement" was able to touch the lives of those they care about with encouraging words in the way I felt my letter did.

Katie

(c)

MAKING A DIFFERENCE AT SCHOOL

The climate of Warren Area High School—about 1,000 students—was deteriorating. Vandalism was up, and someone had recently driven a car across the front yard of the school, leaving deep ruts and prompting the school administration to put up a chain link fence. Parents got together and decided to make a positive difference at the

Work on the school's music rooms included organizing instruments . . .

school. They came up with their own Make a Difference Day (a national event—see www.makeadifferenceday.com on the Web) on a Friday in October 1999. Joan McAfoos and co-coordinator Janet Loranger, along with initiative coordinator Sue Collins, took it from there to develop ideas for projects to improve the school's climate and environment.

In the end, there were about **300** volunteers, **95** projects, and **8–10** students to a project, including all special education students and students that teachers were told to "watch." Some students didn't want to be involved and signed up for a study hall the day of the event, but when they saw what was happening, they asked if they could be assigned a project. Many teachers said they wished they'd scheduled a project for their room after they saw what other teachers came up with (additional projects were planned for the following week).

At one point in the day, a team of workers was cleaning out the sports storage room and found old baseball uniforms. They decided to sell them at a nominal price. By the end of the day, many students were walking around in old uniforms and the student government got the proceeds.

Vandalism has decreased since the event. Young people established new relationships with adults in the community, as well as with each other; some of the students commented on working with other students they never knew, and relationships grew from that experience. The students liked working with teachers and saw that they were real people; it helped foster a different kind of relationship. The students now take pride and ownership in their school.

The beauty of a project like this is twofold. First, it improves the school in a way that everyone can be proud of, and second, it binds together an entire community—teachers working alongside students, parents alongside administrators, businesspeople alongside staff, and so on. The improvements in the school are but a reflection of the improvements in the school community.

Ingredients

Surveys to determine projects

A core group to coordinate projects and entire process

Volunteers to lead groups responsible for completing projects

Contributions of materials and services from local businesses

Instructions

1 Survey the school—adults as well as students—to find out what people would like to do to physically improve the school.

2 Consolidate the list, and enlist parents and other adults in the community—including those without children of their own—to lead the groups responsible for completing each project.

3 Encourage all students to be part of a group. Have them sign up and give their phone numbers.

4 Have the project leaders contact the students, determine what would be needed to complete the project, and plan.

5 Ask local businesses to donate materials or set up registries through which individuals can donate money toward a specific product (e.g., a paintbrush).

6 Encourage all school adults to participate, not only in completing the projects but also in determining what needs to be done—for example, a time line going around the social sciences classroom, wallpaper featuring books on the walls of the language arts classroom, fixing (or affixing) doors to bathroom stalls, painting, putting in plants, or adding artwork both inside and outside the building.

7 Solicit contributions from other businesses (e.g., refreshments).

Chef

Joan McAfoos, *co-coordinator,* Warren Area High School Make a Difference Day, 2077 Conewango Avenue, Warren, PA 16365, 814-723-1871, mcafoos@penn.com

Nutrients

#4—Caring neighborhood, #32—Planning and decision making, #24—Bonding to school

Serves

1,000 students, grades 9–12

Variations

▶ One variation is something Warren Area High School is actually planning: a volunteer day, in which students will write to local charities and ask what they need for one day, then try to accomplish it.

▶ Rather than have a gigantic effort once a year, you can designate several days during the year as "School Improvement Days," on which fewer projects are undertaken but the entire school helps out. Identify tasks beforehand that students with limited abilities can successfully carry out.

. . . and brightening walls with painted musical notes.

♥ PALS

PALS stands for Partners At Lunch Society; it's currently in all 10 San Juan Unified School District high schools and all 10 middle schools; it's planned to be in all 54 elementary schools as well.

The concept (a teacher invites a student to lunch) is simple, but it can reap rich rewards. One teacher invited three "at-risk" students on three different occasions. That Christmas, the three students—independently—went out of their way to buy the teacher gifts, and each—again, independently—acknowledged how much the invitation had meant to them.

Ingredients

> $5/month for each participating teacher or other staff member
> Invitations
> A room to accommodate staff and their student guests
> Food, games, and other items

Instructions

1 Ask staff members to contribute $5 a month to invite a student to lunch.

2 Have the teacher or staff member give the invitation to the student so that they both show up at the designated classroom. Say that they can reward good behavior with an invitation, they can choose a child who seems to need a friend, or they can use other criteria.

3 Each month, set up the classroom with pizza, games, and other activities for half an hour.

4 Introduce everyone at the outset, then involve everyone in an activity; finally, have lunch.

Chef

Maggie Wade, *regional supervisor,* prevention and intervention programs, San Juan Unified School District, 9601 Lake Natoma Drive, Orangevale, CA 95662, 916-986-2236, x330, mwade@mail.sanjuan.edu

Nutrients

#5—Caring school climate, #3—Other adult relationships, #14—Adult role models

Serves

30 students/month/school, grades K–12

Variations

▶ You can formalize the criteria for the invitations, for example, attaining some academic or behavioral milestone, or performing a service for the school community; you can also formalize the invitations (e.g., by involving art classes in creating unique invitations as a class project).

▶ You can make the lunches potlucks, or have the group make the lunch (e.g., salads or sandwiches) together, or, if there's enough time, have the lunches at restaurants.

♥ PLAY FAIR

Here's an example of people observing something extremely typical but then going ahead and doing something wonderful about it. Prairie View Elementary School has about 500 K–5 students, and it was determined that there was too much fighting during recess. The result? Play Fair. Teachers would go out on the playground and give out "tickets" (viewed by the children as a gift, not a summons), whereby the recipients of those tickets would gather in the gymnasium for cooperative play. At first, teachers would focus on students who were either inappropriately aggressive or withdrawn, but they soon expanded the invitations to everyone. Counselor Dawn Donner says that the children love Play Fair and ask for it all during the week.

Ingredients

Ideas for cooperative games and other play (many books and Web sites offer such ideas: for example, see Quicksilver, a book of cooperative games written by Karl Rohnke and published by Kendall/Hunt, 1995; or search for "cooperative games" on a Web search engine)
Facilitators
Time in the gymnasium

Instructions

1 Set aside times in the gymnasium for only cooperative play. For example, on two days of every week, hold two sessions in the gym, 11:15–11:40 and 11:45–12:10.

2 Have teachers choose the students, but be sure that all the students go willingly.

3 Establish rules. No fighting, name-calling, or competition is allowed.

4 Have counselors facilitate the sessions.

Chef

Dawn Donner, *counselor,* Prairie View Elementary School, 300 Soden Drive, Oregon, WI 53575, 608-835-4276

Nutrients

#33—Interpersonal competence, #15—Positive peer influence, #10—Safety

Serves

150 students/week, grades K–5

Variations

▶ You can expand this cooperative, noncompetitive philosophy to the entire school in an effort to change violent, aggressively competitive norms.
▶ You can challenge students to come up with cooperative games that don't require expensive equipment and that everyone can play.

THE READING FAIR

Sheila McChesney-Maher and the 44 young people from her 4-H group have been putting on the Reading Fair for two years now. The beauty of the fair is that families can attend together: Children have fun with various activities, and parents participate in workshops that help them become more involved in their children's reading. Then, during the second half of the fair, the families reunite for more activities and refreshments.

McChesney-Maher's group, ranging from 5 to 17 years old, is involved in virtually every aspect of the fair: coming up with the themes, publicizing the event, making puppets, "adopting" books so that they dress up like the books' main characters and entertain the children, keeping watch over the younger children at the fair, arranging for the parent workshops, and serving refreshments. McChesney-Maher also engaged the services of Solveig Gruber, of the West Virginia Birth-to-Three Regional Educational Services Agency VIII, to show parents how to make books "come alive" for their young children. Regardless of the age of their children, all parents had something to learn at the Reading Fair.

Ingredients

Volunteers

Refreshments

Publicity materials

Two large rooms

Books

Instructions

1 Choose a date and time—say, a two-hour block—for the fair, and publicize it accordingly.

2 Secure at least two large rooms, one for children and the other for adults.

3 Develop short activities for students, K–3, that focus on reading and literacy, for example:

▶ Making bookmarks
▶ Creating books
▶ Listening to descriptions of books by older students dressed as the main characters
▶ Playing word games

4 Develop short workshops for parents that focus on reading and literacy, for example:

▶ Why read to children
▶ How to read to children
▶ How to make books "come alive"

Provide examples of good books to read as well as resources for reading to children.

5 Develop an hour-long block of family activities, for example, puppet shows and refreshments.

6 Solicit participation from local elementary schools, libraries, bookstores, Head Start and day-care programs, and other places with access to young children.

7 When families show up at the fair, have volunteers on hand to take charge of the children and to usher the parents into the workshops.

Chef

Sheila McChesney-Maher, *leader,* Slanesville Rise-N-Shine 4-H, RR #1, Box 65B, Augusta, WV 26704, mntnlady@citlink.net

Nutrients

#6—Parent involvement in schooling, #8—Youth as resources, #25—Reading for pleasure

Serves

At least 60 families

Variations

▶ You can expand the fair to appeal to young people of all ages.

▶ You can have one workshop that could be attended by both parents and their children, so the parents might work on reading techniques they recently learned.

STRENGTH INTERVIEWS

Strength interviews epitomize asset-based thinking. In New Richmond High School, New Richmond, Wisconsin, they're used formally as part of freshmen interviews—sessions in which counselors put faces to the names of incoming students, usually about 200. In addition, school counselor Kelly Curtis uses them at the conclusion of all her counseling sessions with students. "It gets them thinking about what's right instead of what's wrong," she says. "They leave in a different frame of mind." Students, says Curtis, don't usually have a difficult time answering the questions; frequently, the responses are somewhat interconnected. Most of them cite "whos" (their family or friends) or "whats" (their jobs or hobbies) as "protectors"; many of them list their approachability or friendliness as inner resources. The idea, says Curtis, is to show them how to choose their own attitude about themselves, and to focus on the positive rather than the negative.

Ingredients

Counselors

Instructions

1 Write on a sheet of paper the following three questions:

▶ "Who protects you, or who has protected you?"
▶ "What protects you, or what has protected you?"
▶ "What inner resources or strengths do you have?"

2 Use these questions as a basis for pointing out students' strengths in at least the following situations:

▶ During interviews of incoming freshmen
▶ At the conclusion of all counseling sessions

Chef

Kelly Curtis, *school counselor*, New Richmond High School, 701 East 11th Street, New Richmond, WI 54017, 715-243-7451

Nutrients

#40—Positive view of personal future, #37—Personal power, #16—High expectations

Serves

Students, grades 9–12

Variations

▶ You can have each student respond to the questions—either in an interview or on paper—at the beginning of the year and then use those responses to guide future discussions.
▶ You can have school staff also respond to the questions, for example, in job interviews or evaluations.

WALK YOUR CHILD TO SCHOOL DAY

For communities in which many families live close to the school, this activity works wonderfully well. In the Fort Collins, Colorado, area, six to eight elementary schools participate—about 2,000 people. Athletes from nearby Colorado State University contribute by talking to the students and their families when they arrive. It's also a good opportunity to talk about assets.

Ingredients

Snacks
Information for families

Instructions

1 Set one day aside—say, in September—to be Walk Your Child to School Day; publicize the event.

2 Have snacks, such as juice and breakfast bars, ready for families when they arrive.

3 Provide safety information as well as information about developmental assets.

Chef

Ruth Lytle-Barnaby, *director of community and foundation development,* Poudre Valley Health System, 1024 South Lemay Avenue, Fort Collins, CO 80525, 970-495-7512

Nutrients

#1—Family support, #6—Parent involvement in schooling, #2—Positive family communication

Serves

2,000 students, grades K–6, and their parents

Variations

▶ You can modify Walk Your Child to School Day on the basis of your families' needs. It could be Walk Your Child Home from School Day or Walk Your Child to School Saturday or even Walk Your Child to School Tuesday Evening. The two latter options would necessitate your arranging some sort of event at the school to draw people there.

▶ Extend the morning to be an open house at the school, in which parents experience their children's morning routines.

THE WALL OF ASSETS

This activity, created by Amy Coldwall, has been disseminated by Helen Beattie, who works with the Vermont Rural Partnership. Beattie assists rural schools with implementing and interpreting *Search Institute Profiles of Student Life: Attitudes and Behaviors,* the self-report survey developed expressly to measure the extent to which students in grades 6–12 have the 40 developmental assets. She has put activities such as this one into a manual called "A Guide for Student Analysis of the Search Institute Data: Organization of a Day Retreat for 6th- through 12th-Graders."

Vermont's Coventry Village School, a small (125 students, grades K–8) rural school, used the Wall of Assets to its advantage several years ago. It came out in the survey, and in subsequent discussions among the 25 7th- and 8th-grade students, that the 7th-grade students were somewhat irked by the 8th-grade students: The latter seemingly received many more privileges and were perceived as treating their underclassmates as second-class school citizens. This surprised Principal Pam Macy, who, apart from the discussion, says she never would have picked up on the difficulties the 7th-grade students were having.

The discussions that arose from the Wall of Assets led to the 7th-grade students' setting up a two-day leadership camp—arranging, among other things, food, vendors, chaperones, and activities—for both them and the 8th-grade students and effected some change in school policies as well. Because of the survey, the Wall of Assets activity, the discussions, and the ensuing leadership camp, the students are now more aware of each other's strengths and needs.

Ingredients

40 plastic or cardboard building blocks
8–10 pads of adhesive notes

Instructions

1 Build a "wall of assets" with 40 plastic or cardboard blocks, each block labeled with an asset (perhaps with colors designating categories).

2 Show students the wall and describe the assets (as well as the metaphor).

3 Remove several blocks and say that the wall can still be strong without all 40 assets; then remove more until the wall tumbles. Say that at some point young people need a minimum of assets, and that number differs for each person.

4 Arrange students into small groups; give each group asset blocks and a pad of adhesive notes. Ask students to cover each block with as many examples of that asset in their school and community as they can.

5 After about 20 minutes, reconvene the large group and ask students from each group to reconstruct the wall with the blocks by explaining the assets and the examples they chose for each one.

6 When the wall is once again complete, ask students what they think about it. Reinforce the number of assets that are present in their lives, and remark on which assets need to be further built.

Chefs

Amy Coldwall, *school psychologist,* and **Helen Beattie,** Vermont Rural Partnership, P.O. Box 37, East Hardwick, VT 05836, 802-472-6846, hnbeattie@aol.com

Nutrients

#40—Positive view of personal future, #29—Honesty, #37—Personal power

Serves

25 students, grades 7–8

Variations

▶ You can expand this to a schoolwide activity, giving different classrooms responsibility for placing assets—or asset categories—in the wall.

▶ You can make this into a play, in which each asset—or asset category—can be a skit put on by students to illustrate how the assets are built; you can even invite family members to participate in the play.

 EXTRA HELPINGS for *The Wall of Assets: Excerpt from the guide for student analysis of data (by Helen Beattie; copyright 2000 by the Vermont Department of Education; used by permission).*

▶ Rationale for Student Anaylsis ◀

Student analysis of the Search Institute's survey on developmental assets, *Profiles of Student Life: Attitudes and Behaviors*, presents an ideal opportunity to put youth "out-in-front" in building assets for their school and community. The data reflect the voice of youth. It is therefore only appropriate that these same young people bring life and meaning to *their* numbers.

Students are too often the recipients of well-intended adult-driven decisions about their health and well-being. The implicit message is that they are not capable of being leaders and participants in positively shaping the world in which they live. Hopeless and disempowered youth are all too prevalent in our schools and communities because this message is given and reinforced repeatedly in our culture. We want young people to be prepared to be active citizens in our democracy, yet we provide few meaningful opportunities to make decisions which will significantly impact their lives and others, thereby building these life skills.

The Search Institute survey data and school and community mobilization process provide an ideal opportunity to change this message. When young people become the messengers for the data and how it can influence a future direction for the community at large, adults are presented with a compelling opportunity to value youth for their honesty, commitment, wisdom, vision, and capacity to shape a better future for us all.

A summary, as determined by the 7th and 8th graders, of the data of the five major strengths and five major concerns found in the Coventry Village School community (all percentages and comments have been taken directly from the students' summaries):

STRENGTHS

1. **People feel safe in town**—Young people feel safe at home, at school, and in the neighborhood.
   Results: Yes, 85%; No, 8%; Sometimes, 8%
   Summary: We feel pretty safe in town. Almost everybody seems safe at home.

2. **Two-plus hours in sports per week**—Young people spend three or more hours per week in sports, clubs, or organizations at school or in the community.
   Results: Yes, 67%; No, 29%; Sometimes, 4%
   Summary: The people think it is important to do two or more hours a week.

3. **Feel safe at home**—Young people feel safe at home, at school, and in the neighborhood.
   Results: Yes, 92%; No, 4%; Sometimes, 4%
   Summary: Almost everybody seems safe at home.

4. **Alcohol use**—Young people believe it is important not to be sexually active or to use alcohol or other drugs.
   Results: Yes, 58%; No, 4%; Sometimes, 37%
   Summary: We're not tempted to do sex and drugs.

5. **Honest to self**—Young people "tell the truth even when it is not easy."
   Results: Yes, 83%; No, 8%; Sometimes, 8%
   Summary: We're honest for ourselves, but we're loyal to our friends.

CONCERNS

1. **Positive family communication**—belief that young person and her or his parent(s) communicate positively, and young person is willing to seek advice and counsel from parent(s).
   Results: Yes, 53%; No, 4%; Sometimes, 43%
   Summary: Means kids do better in school; it gives you confidence; you get to school in a better mood. So this needs to be more for students.

2. **Safety**—Young people feel safe at school.
   Results: Yes, 80% 8th-graders, 50% 7th-graders; No, 0% 8th-graders; 40% 7th-graders; Sometimes, 20% 8th-graders; 10% 7th-graders
   Summary: Most of the 8th-graders feel safe at school, but only half the 7th-graders feel safe. Eighth-graders tend to "lord" it over 7th-graders by tradition.

3. **Youth programs, weekend activities**—Young person has activities in sports, clubs, or organizations at school or in the community on the weekends.
   Results: Yes, 53%; No, 42%; Sometimes, 5%
   Summary: Not much going on, on the weekends. We think that the percent is not high enough.

4. **Positive view of personal future**—Young people are optimistic about their personal future.
   Results: Yes, 56%; No, 13%; Sometimes, 28%; Only 46% think this is important.
   Summary: Students believe that more students should think it is important to want to have a positive view of the future. They are concerned that more than half don't even think it is important.

5. **Self-esteem**—Young people report having a high self-esteem.
   Results: Yes, 25% 8th-graders, 66% 7th-graders; No, 25% 8th-graders, 8% 7th-graders; Sometimes, 50% 8th-graders, 25% 7th-graders
   Summary: We think that not enough people have self-esteem, and it's important.

Main Courses

MAIN COURSES are programs and practices that require some coordination to be effective. They usually need a good monitoring system to make sure that everything is being implemented as planned, and they may entail cooperation from major sections of the school. The upside to all this is twofold: The effects of such programs can be particularly deep, broad, and long-lasting; and such programs can help to establish a framework to encompass other asset-building activities.

▶ *The Recipes* ◀

Asset Ambassadors *(Maine)*

Celebrate the Child Day *(Kentucky)*

The Community Chest *(Missouri)*

A Community Taking the Initiative *(Florida)*

The Family Resource Room *(Michigan)*

The Farm *(California)*

IMPACT *(Iowa)*

Kids Helping Neighbors *(Indiana)*

Neighborhood Youth Councils *(Pennsylvania)*

The Orion Program *(Montana)*

The School of Clubs *(Mississippi)*

Steppin' Up to Solutions *(New York)*

Strengths in Families *(Alaska)*

Student-Led Conferences *(Wyoming)*

Upstairs *(North Dakota)*

Vocations On-Site *(Delaware)*

ASSET AMBASSADORS

The structure reflected in Asset Ambassadors keeps growing. The "community conversations" described below—there were 33 of them in Portland—eventually metamorphosed into a citywide meeting of over 350 participants, cofacilitated by an adult and a teenager. An alliance was forged between the Portland School Committee and the City Council, and as a result, for the first time, the City Council unanimously passed a measure calling for a Youth Advisory Council—14 young people, 5 elected and 9 appointed.

The council is now planning many kinds of projects: a teen job bank, where jobs could be brokered with both small and large businesses; community policing centers, where teenagers could drop in and get information and support; and a program in which middle school students would build window boxes (the materials donated by the police) and then provide them at low or no cost to residents in housing projects for the elderly.

The key, says Mike Clifford, a major coordinator of these efforts, has been to set up a community structure that is long-lasting—deep and wide.

Ingredients

Access to schools and municipal agencies
One or two adult advisers from each school

Instructions

1 Give awareness presentations about the developmental assets framework to school adults at staff meetings.

2 Conduct an outreach for "student asset ambassadors": Ask the high schools, the middle schools, the vocational-technical schools, and the alternative schools to choose 12–15 students to be ambassadors.

3 Hold short meetings with these ambassadors, and one or two adult advisers, at each school to tell them about the assets and about *Search Institute Profiles of Student Life: Attitudes and Behaviors*, the self-report survey that measures the extent to which students in grades 6–12 have the 40 developmental assets. (You don't have to use the survey in order to do this activity. You can find summaries of survey data in such Search Institute books as *A Fragile Foundation: The State of Developmental Assets among American Youth* and *Great Places to Learn: How Asset-Building Schools Help Students Succeed*, and use those summaries as starting points for discussions.)

4 Ask the ambassadors to go to classes in their school, to assemblies, and to other gatherings to talk about the assets and garner support for the survey or for initiating asset-building activities.

5 After the survey has been implemented and scored, have the ambassadors recruit others for "community conversations"—groups cofacilitated by an adult and a teenager in three two-hour sessions; the agenda of the sessions is first, explaining developmental assets and the asset framework; second, reporting and interpreting the survey results; and third, inviting suggestions on a course of action.

Chef

Mike Clifford, *coordinator,* Safe and Drug-Free Schools Program, Portland Public Schools, 331 Veranda Street, Portland, ME 04103, 207-874-8100, x3026

Nutrients

#15—Positive peer influence, #7—Community values youth, #8—Youth as resources

Serves

12–15 students, grades 6–12

Variations

▶ You can make use of local media outlets to publicize the "community conversations," as well as the asset framework.

▶ You can facilitate similar dynamics in elementary schools by establishing asset ambassadors on a schoolwide basis.

 EXTRA HELPINGS for *Asset Ambassadors: Excerpt from the discussion guide for community conversations.*

▶ **Discussion Questions** ◀

Discussion questions from Session One, What helps us be our best? (The purpose of this session was to talk about the people and experiences that helped participants to be their best.)

1. What are (or were) the people and experiences that you have (or had) as a young person that make (or made) a positive difference in your life? What is (or was) it about those people and experiences that helped you?
2. In what ways do you think our community or your neighborhood supports young people today?
3. In what ways do you think our community or your neighborhood falls short in supporting young people?
4. In this community, how do kids and adults get along? What do you see and experience?
5. When you think of "assets" that young people need to be healthy and whole, what comes to your mind?

Discussion questions from Session Two, What are kids saying? (The purpose of this session was to talk about the results of the survey that was given to sixth through twelfth graders in Portland.)

1. As you looked at the results of the survey, what surprised you? Why did they surprise you?
2. What did not surprise you? Why didn't they surprise you?
3. Did you see any patterns or trends?
4. Given the results of the survey, what do you see as the most urgent needs of Portland's kids today?
5. Why isn't every child in Portland experiencing all

40 assets in their lives? What do you think some of the root causes might be that explain the absence of assets?

Discussion questions from Session Three, What can we do? (The purpose of this session was to talk about things that participants could do, as individuals and as a community, to build the assets that kids needed in Portland.)

1. What actions could we take that would have an immediate, positive impact on the lives of Portland's kids?
   - As individuals
   - As groups (businesses, congregations, schools, etc.)
   - As members of a neighborhood
   - On a citywide level

2. What actions could we take that would have a positive impact on the lives of Portland's kids over the next 3–6 months?
   - As individuals
   - As groups
   - As members of a neighborhood
   - On a citywide level

3. What actions could we take over the long term?
   - As individuals
   - As groups
   - As members of a neighborhood
   - On a citywide level

4. What resources do we need to make these things happen?

CELEBRATE THE CHILD DAY

They are a poor community in Kentucky—Ohio County, about 20,000 people—but their community-school partnership comprises several hundred active members. Everything, including community education, mentoring, drug education, and student assistance, is now under the banner of this partnership. Every year, on a Saturday in the middle of April, they have a fair that they call Celebrate the Child Day. The fair is in its eighth year, and for the past three years, the theme has been asset building. About 3,000 people attended last year, and 50 organizations were represented; it's the biggest day around.

The theme started when students were asked what they wanted to do about the fact that they didn't feel the community cared about them, and they suggested making developmental assets the theme of the fair. After each fair, students as young as kindergartners clamor to participate in the next one.

Ingredients

Representatives from community organizations
Signs or sandwich boards highlighting assets
Student volunteers to work at the fair

Instructions

1 Recruit about 60 high school students and middle school students to work at the fair.

2 Solicit contributions from organizations in the community (e.g., businesses, hospitals, and youth-serving organizations).

3 Write the names of the assets on signs or sandwich boards, and have students walk around with them, explaining to people what the assets are and why they're important.

4 Focus the events—puppet shows, readings, face painting, musical exhibitions—on young people, and specifically on assets.

Chef

James Robinson, *director,* Together We Care, 100 West Render Street, Suite 1, Hartford, KY 42347, 270-298-7744, jrobinso@ohio.k12.ky.us

Nutrients

#7—Community values youth, #8—Youth as resources, #13—Neighborhood boundaries

Serves

An entire community

Variations

▶ You can augment the activities with themes of interest to young people, for example, the influences of media or the pressures to be popular.
▶ You can feature discussions on how the community can help young people and how young people in turn can help the community.

THE COMMUNITY CHEST

The Community Chest is a central repository for donations from businesses around Cape Girardeau, Missouri. It began because most of the mentors in the community were college students with limited funds to spend on the young people they were mentoring. With the donations—so far about 300 businesses have signed up—the young people being mentored will have opportunities to participate in a variety of fun, interactive, and educational activities previously unavailable to them. An adjunct to the Community Chest is a "bank" of donated sports equipment (e.g., skates, bicycles, canoes, tents, basketballs, baseballs, bats and gloves, helmets, pads), again donated by local businesses. Mentors can check out the equipment for themselves and the young people they're helping.

Ingredients

Publicity
Donations from community businesses
A repository for all the donations
Coordination of resources

Instructions

1 Solicit donations in the form of coupons, discounts, and so on, from local businesses (e.g., theaters, restaurants, barbers, video stores, bookstores, and entertainment centers).

2 Collect the donations in a central "community chest," for example, at a school or community center.

3 Make the donations available to mentors from established groups in the community (e.g., Big Brothers Big Sisters).

4 Publicize the program with an area-wide media campaign so that businesses continue to donate and mentors continue to use the donations.

Chef

Leah Shrum, *prevention advocate,* Community 2000 Substance Abuse Prevention Resource Center, 343 Academic, Mail Stop 3970, Southeast Missouri State University, Cape Girardeau, MO 63701, 573-651-5153

Nutrients

#4—Caring neighborhood, #3—Other adult relationships, #7—Community values youth

Serves

Students, grades K–12

Variations

▶ You can give certificates to local businesses that they can display as both an acknowledgment of their contribution and publicity for the program.
▶ You can do this activity just as easily if you're involved with a school-based mentoring program; you can encourage students and school adults to collect donations.

A COMMUNITY TAKING THE INITIATIVE

The Healthy Community Initiative is focused on Winter Park High School, Winter Park, Florida, but the partners include the Winter Park Foundation and a training company, Neptune, Green & Associates. In October 1998, youth were predominant in a two-hour forum for about 250 people from throughout the community to discuss the developmental assets framework and the specific strengths and needs of the students. In 1999, the students put together an intergenerational leadership team, which included philanthropists, to promote asset-building activities.

Currently, a 15-member team at the high school is trying to improve the physical environment and also helping students who transfer to the school to adjust more comfortably. In nearby West Winter Park, a low-income neighborhood, girls designed a technical center, made a PowerPoint presentation promoting the center, and are now setting it up. Other activities throughout the community are being pursued by a variety of groups spawned by the initiative.

Ray Larsen, the executive director of the initiative, tells about a youth attending one of the meetings and a teacher later saying that the youth was "blown away" because she realized that adults in the community really did care about her and other youth. He tells another story in which a woman was walking around the neighborhood telling her husband about assets when they passed some young people playing basketball. She said that she realized the only times she noticed the kids were when they were making noise. "Thanks for reminding me that we don't have to change the world," she told Larsen. "We just have to change ourselves a little bit."

Ingredients

People committed to learning about and promoting the developmental assets framework

Search Institute Profiles of Student Life: Attitudes and Behaviors *self-report survey*

Instructions

1 Arrange your area into consortia, reflected in a high school and its feeder schools (those middle schools and junior high schools from which graduating students will enter the high school)—a "naturally forming community."

2 Train core faculty and other staff in the asset framework; they in turn can go into their communities to do "community capacity building"—helping the community find its own resources to build assets. The first step is to identify key individuals who are committed to helping young people build assets.

3 These people then form leadership groups; thus, there is a "subtle passing of roles," a shift of ownership, from the main initiative to the smaller communities.

4 The leadership groups may then decide to implement the *Search Institute Profiles of Student Life: Attitudes and Behaviors* self-report survey that measures the extent to which students in grades 6–12 have the 40 developmental assets; the results of the survey can be used as a catapult for further activities.

Chefs

Sydney Green, *partner,* Neptune, Green & Associates, Winter Park, Florida; **Ray Larsen,** *executive director,* Healthy Community Initiative of Greater Orlando, 507 East Michigan Street, Orlando, FL 32806, 407-649-6891, hciflorida.org

Nutrients

#8—Youth as resources, #7—Community values youth, #37—Personal power

Serves

An entire community

Variations

▶ You can choose the areas in which you want to begin your initiative, for example, middle schools/junior high schools. If you live in a small or rural community, your task is even easier; you can focus on one or two areas.

▶ You can use the PTA to spread information about the asset framework throughout the community; you can send representatives to businesses as well, asking to speak to their employees about what they can do as parents and as citizens of the community.

THE FAMILY RESOURCE ROOM

After research-based presentations made by concerned parents from the Family Resource Institute, the school board included in its blueprint for a new school a Family Resource Room. The room is open to students (about 1,500) and families in the community from 7 A.M. to 10 P.M. Paid staff are there from 25 to 40 hours a week, and about 150 volunteers, including members of Ameri-Corps, help out as well. The room is booked 75 percent of the time.

The thrust of this activity, of course, isn't *how to acquire* a family resource room; rather, it's *how to use* a family resource room. In this case, the community of Ishpeming, Michigan, came together to create a room that actively involved parents in their students' schooling and at the same time contributed to a caring school climate.

Ingredients

A large room in a school—bigger than a classroom but smaller than a gymnasium
Kitchen appliances
Media equipment
Software, toys, books
A checkout system
Staff

Instructions

1 Stock the room with a photocopier, two PCs with Internet access, TV/VCR, overhead projector and screen, reading chairs/book nook, dry-erase board, refrigerator, microwave oven, coffeemakers, and sink/drinking fountain area.

2 Make available software, toys, board books, and other materials that families can check out.

3 Let students and families know that anyone can come into the Family Resource Room at any time to be with students or do some other tasks. For example, middle school students can come in and research books and other resources, tutor younger kids, clean up, and otherwise help out.

4 Staff the room from about 8:30 A.M. to 3 P.M. every day, but keep it open for use the same hours as the building is open, i.e., from 7 in the morning to 10 in the evening.

Chef

Debra Asano, *special services coordinator,* NICE Community School District, 350 Aspen Ridge School Road, Ishpeming, MI 49849, 906-485-3177

Nutrients

#6—Parent involvement in schooling, #5—Caring school climate, #24—Bonding to school

Serves

900 students, grades K–8

Variations

▶ You can set aside days—or hours of days—in which certain groups have priority for use of the room; you can even make volunteering in the room the "price" for using it.
▶ You can solicit contributions from families to improve the room; focus, however, on the safety and security of the room rather than the equipment and materials.

 **See EXTRA HELPINGS**

EXTRA HELPINGS for *The Family Resource Room: Positive responses about the room, from a survey of elementary school teachers.*

Please tell us what the existence of the Family Resource Room has meant for you.

- Helped me out a lot with class preparation.
- A place for parents to go, especially beginning of year with separation anxiety of new students.
- Have borrowed many materials and used the room to extend class activities.
- Our parents have a place to feel "at home."
- A comfortable place for parents to feel they belong and are a part of the school.
- Warm, friendly addition to school.
- It's made for a more positive atmosphere for those who want to become more involved in their child's education. Parents are far more willing to volunteer because I feel they have a place to call their own.
- Parents are more involved in school activities.

Please tell us what it does/has done for the school district.

- Parents feel more positive about school now. More have volunteered.
- Extended the school to the community
- I believe the Family Resource Room has built a strong school/community bridge.
- Given us much positive PR (newspaper, TV, word of mouth)!
- It's made parents feel welcome and has encouraged parents to become involved. Great public relations. Parents feel like they're cared about!
- Parent involvement results in positive communications, support, and a team concept between home and school!

🍎 THE FARM

Ohlone Elementary School, in Palo Alto, California, is a public elementary school with about 400 students in grades K–5. With its philosophical roots in experiential, project-based learning, in 1984 it turned an acre of land into a farm, with animals, a meadow, and gardens. The farm is cared for by the entire school community, culminating in a fall harvest festival. The students, who are taught to relate their learning to issues and problems in the real world, are inextricably entwined with the progress of the farm. For example, in 1992, students saved the pond from stagnation by conducting research, determining the water capacity, testing the water, and deciding which kinds of filters, pumps, and plants were necessary to maintain a reliable flow of clean water. To this day, students return to the school to check on the health of the pond.

Marianna Keller, parent volunteer and chairwoman of the Ohlone Farm Council, illustrates the wonder of the farm by relating the story of how she and a young child—perhaps a 4th or 5th grader—shared an intelligent conversation one weekend while shoveling manure into compost heaps. They were discussing how the smelly manure changed into rather sweet-smelling compost, but they were talking more or less as equals; the relationship was an honest one, without control or hierarchy. Keller was struck by the force of that interaction, and she subsequently noted that such relationships on the farm were not uncommon.

The farm is a great example of school engagement to the max. Students take an active part in their own learning—not because it's assigned, not because their grade depends on it, but because they're genuinely interested in it. The responsibility they assume for that learning isn't a burden but quite the opposite: It's an uplifting force that spurs them to learn more.

Ingredients

A parcel of land
Animals
Gardens
Professional workers
Volunteers
Coordination between farm activities and a core curriculum

Harvest at the farm includes vegetables and conversation.

Instructions

1 Transform land on school grounds or adjacent to or near the school into a farm or garden that includes any of the following:
- ▶ Goats, chickens, sheep, or rabbits, with housing
- ▶ A pond, with ducks and fish
- ▶ A meadow (or prairie or grove of trees)
- ▶ A garden
- ▶ A fence around the land

2 Use a combination of hired farm aides, school staff, parents, and students to take care of the animals, maintain the meadow, plant and tend the garden, and do the other chores necessary to keep the farm going; for example:

▶ Five older students paired with five younger students can work three 10-minute shifts a day to let the animals out and feed them (first shift in the morning), clean up after them (second shift at recess), and put them back in their housing (third shift after school).

▶ Each class can be allotted a row in the garden, and students can plant whatever they wish in their row—vegetables, herbs, flowers, and so on.

▶ Families or neighboring residents can help take care of the farm on weekends, at holidays, and during the summer.

▶ A farm aide can coordinate the farm.

The school sheep

3 Tie in curricula with the farm, for example:

▶ Learning about patterns and distances by laying out a plan for the garden

▶ Learning about chemistry and biology by keeping the pond free of algae

▶ Learning about different cultures by growing (and cooking) foods eaten by those cultures

▶ Learning about the cycles of life by observing the animals and plants on the farm

Chef

Marianna Keller, *chairwoman,* Farm Council, Ohlone Elementary School, 950 Amarillo Street, Palo Alto, CA 94303, 650-856-1726 (W), www.ohlone.palo-alto.ca.us

Nutrients

#22—School engagement, #3—Other adult relationships, #30—Responsibility

Serves

400 students, grades K–5

Variations

▶ This may seem daunting to some schools—particularly those in parts of the country with short growing seasons or arid climates. But you can accomplish similar goals on a much smaller scale, for example, by having only a garden (which can produce vegetables that students can then eat!), or by having something larger that you can tend with other schools or nearby residents. You can even grow things in the classroom; that will still provide students with an opportunity to be caring and responsible.

▶ You can "adopt" a nearby farm or garden and allow students to visit it in order to apply what they've learned in the classroom.

▶ *Incorporating the Farm into the Curriculum* ◀

SEPTEMBER	Introduce the farm, farm chores, and animals to children; prepare beds for winter; sedimentation experiment; worm composting
OCTOBER	Composting; what makes a pile "hot"; compost critters; additives; Harvest Festival; planting cover crops; herbs
NOVEMBER	Plant bulbs; learn about tools, clean and sharpen them; anatomy of chickens and turkeys
DECEMBER	Force indoor bulbs, soil testing; animal anatomy; how weather affects the farm; tree anatomy
JANUARY	Plan gardens; look at seed catalogs; introduction to the greenhouse; heat mats; soil temperature; hydroponics
FEBRUARY	Start seeds in flats; plant anatomy; introduction to fertilizer; fertilize fruit trees; prune trees
MARCH	Double-dig beds; compost cover crops; test soil and fertilize beds; insect anatomy; beneficial/harmful insects—a hunt and survey of different locations
APRIL	Plant/start seeds directly in the ground; set up row covers; pond—what is in the pond, how the filters work; what really lives in the pond, using a microscope to investigate pond critters; why things float or sink
MAY	Thin fruit trees and look for evidence of garden pests; natural repellents; different types of weeds—identification, how to prevent them, why they are good/bad; check in with the compost pile to determine readiness; water and mix; start transplants
JUNE	Transplant all greenhouse plants; stake tomatoes; make paper; learn about making a terrarium; end-of-the-year farm party

Other areas of learning: taking responsibility for nurturing living things; overcoming fear of animals; developing caring relationships with animals and plants; deriving things from animals (e.g., eggs, wool); learning where food comes from; recognizing what it takes to complete a job; using tools and equipment responsibly; cooperating; appreciating the value of hard work; acquiring scientific observation skills; understanding cycles; having fun playing outdoors in a natural setting

⬛ IMPACT

IMPACT stands for Informing More People about Alcohol, Cannabis, and Tobacco. Seven high schools in the Cedar Rapids, Iowa, area are involved, and so far about 20 students design and deliver presentations on drugs and drug use to schools and groups throughout the community. Barbara Gay, director of prevention services, says that they're thinking of removing the stipend from the program; students tell her that the money isn't important, and a few have refused to accept it.

Ingredients

> *Information and activities relating to drugs and*
> *drug use*
> *Trainers for students, and a place to facilitate the*
> *training*
> *Liaisons among schools and community groups*
> *Nominal stipends (optional)*

Instructions

1 Ask high school counselors to identify students who would be interested in and capable of making presentations about drug use.

2 Invite the students and give them training—say, 12 hours' worth, at evening sessions—in issues relating to drugs (specifically, alcohol, marijuana, and tobacco) and drug use.

3 Offer each student $50 for completing the training, $5 for making a presentation, and $7 for participating in three-hour monthly update meetings held in the evenings at rotating locations in the school district.

4 Give students opportunities to design their own presentations, lasting about 45 minutes, and including demonstrations, puppets, skits, and discussions. Have them focus on drugs, drug use, making good decisions, and resisting negative peer pressure.

5 Coordinate presentations at elementary schools, middle schools, and community groups. Have one adult accompany one to three students at each presentation.

Chef

Barbara Gay, *director of prevention services,* Area Substance Abuse Council, 3601 16th Avenue SW, Cedar Rapids, IA 52404, 319-390-4611

Nutrients

#31—Restraint, #15—Positive peer influence, #35—Resistance skills

Serves

20 students, grades 9–12

Variations

▶ This is obviously a structure that you can use for a variety of topics (e.g., HIV/AIDS prevention, violence prevention, and training in social skills) and with students of all ages.

▶ Instead of having students make presentations, you can give them opportunities to teach a multi-day course (e.g., 10 lessons over a two-month period).

KIDS HELPING NEIGHBORS

"Keep it simple." That's what kindergarten teacher Julie Moore says about her activity to teach children about caring for their neighbors. And this is a very simple project, but I've listed it as a "main course" because for these children, it *is* a main course. Caring for one's neighbors is not a onetime event; as Moore says, "Community help is something you can do your whole life." That's the lesson she hopes her students learn from this activity.

An important component of this activity is the emphasis on the family; it's the family who participates together —replacing the batteries in an elderly neighbor's smoke detectors, painting a single neighbor's picnic table, helping a teenage neighbor move firewood, bringing a grieving neighbor fresh-picked flowers and homemade cookies. The simplicity of Moore's assignment belies its richness—for the children, their families, and their neighbors.

Ingredients

Access to families

Instructions

1 Discuss with students what it means to help neighbors and how people can offer help.

2 Assign students the task of doing something special for a neighbor of any age (brainstorm ideas if students can't come up with anything), with these criteria:

▶ It must be done with a member of the student's family.

▶ Students need to present what they did on a single page; the page can contain a photograph, illustrations, writing, or a combination.

3 Contact students' family members to let them know of the assignment.

4 When students have done their assignments and brought in their pages, assemble them into a book and show the book to all the students.

5 Discuss with students how they can continue doing caring things for their neighbors.

Chef

Julie Moore, *teacher*, Riverview Elementary School, 513 Buckingham Drive, Marion, IN 46952, 765-662-2427

Nutrients

#26—Caring, #2—Positive family communication, #20—Time at home

Serves

32 students, kindergarten

Variations

▶ You can do this activity with other grade levels, and you can increase the sophistication of the "product," for example, by requiring written reports or creative projects.

▶ You can do this activity on a regular basis to reinforce the idea that caring is a continual activity.

 **See EXTRA HELPINGS**

EXTRA HELPINGS for *Kids Helping Neighbors: Pages from the book made by the children to record their helpful deeds vividly show the impact of this activity.*

my brother and I painted a picnic table for our neighbor friend. He gave us our own paint brushes and our own can of paint each. We had a great time doing that for our neighbor.

Tommy E.

NEIGHBORHOOD YOUTH COUNCILS

Milton Hershey School, in Hershey, Pennsylvania, is a private residential school, divided into elementary, middle, high, elementary/middle, and middle/high grade levels; the school serves about 1,200 young people from more than 30 states. The students come from disadvantaged families and are referred by families as well as youth-serving organizations. They live in 109 homes, 8–12 young people to a home, with a certified, married couple acting as houseparents. The homes are arranged in five neighborhoods, about 20 homes to a neighborhood. The young people's parents or guardians visit on weekends, holidays, and other times during the year.

The administrators of Milton Hershey School have explicitly adopted an asset-building framework in both structure and deed. The residents are governed through a network of councils in which young people are chosen to make decisions and act as a liaison between themselves and the adults. A major leadership team of four young people shares responsibilities over the neighborhood.

Replicating the Hershey organizational structure exactly will be beyond the capabilities of most schools; but replicating parts of it—and the spirit of it—is, in many school communities, certainly doable.

At Hershey, a new school center has just been built, and Barry Sloane, director of student programs, says that assets "are everywhere. We really believe in assets."

Ingredients

Organizational structure
Time to plan
Adult advisers

Instructions

1 Consider the Hershey homes as classrooms; instead of 8–12 young people in a home, there might be 25–30 students in a classroom.

2 Consider the Hershey neighborhoods as grade levels; instead of 20 homes to a neighborhood, there might be 20 classrooms to a grade level.

3 Each home has a primary representative and an alternate. Twice a month, these 20 representatives participate in a neighborhood meeting that lasts about two hours. There they might plan activities like service projects or cultural events.

Similarly, each classroom might have a primary representative and an alternate (perhaps rotated as a privilege as well as a responsibility). Twice a month, these representatives might participate in a grade-level meeting that lasts about two hours. There they might plan activities like service projects or cultural events.

4 On Tuesday evenings, each home has a "Family Meeting," in which the representatives report on their discussions in the neighborhood meetings.

Similarly, on Tuesday afternoons, each classroom might have a "Class Meeting," in which the representatives might report on their discussions in the grade-level meetings.

5 About six times a year, all 109 representatives meet in the full Neighborhood Youth Council, again, for about two hours. At these meetings, they might break into neighborhoods or plan schoolwide events.

Similarly, all the classroom representatives might meet in a full School Youth Council, and at these meetings they might break into grade levels or plan schoolwide events.

6 Planning is rotated among the neighborhoods, just as planning might be rotated among the grade levels. Full agendas are followed in all meetings.

7 In addition to this, neighborhoods nominate four young people for the "leadership team." These people have to submit applications and then are chosen to be on the team. Again, each grade level might nominate four students for its "leadership team."

8 In all these meetings and planning sessions—and Hershey also has a student council, which addresses traditional school issues—the adults are primarily advisers; they encourage proposals for projects, but they leave most of the work to the young people.

9 The houseparents have an advisory group, too. They identify adult leaders among them, and then they in turn plan different events. (For example, this will be the third year of the neighborhood Olympics. It's held on Columbus Day, when about half the school remains on campus. Each neighborhood has its own shirts and banners. There's an opening ceremony, and the Olympics features both athletic and nonathletic—for example, quiz bowl, karaoke—competitions.) School adults can also identify adult leaders among them, and these adults can plan different events.

Chef

Barry Sloane, *director of student programs,* Milton Hershey School, P.O. Box 830, Hershey, PA 17033, 717-520-2071, sloaneb@mhs-pa.org

Nutrients

#30—Responsibility, #8—Youth as resources, #37—Personal power

Serves

1,200 students, pre-K–12

Variations

▶ As suggested, you can adapt this organizational structure to the makeup of an individual school. One variation is to have crossover between grade levels, so that older and younger students are working together. Safeguards—boundaries, expectations—may need to be implemented to prevent the younger students from being intimidated, but the dynamic should prove productive.

▶ You can also set up committees across grade levels, so, for example, students interested in community service or disciplinary procedures or drug policy can hear from their schoolmates in different grades.

▶ Goals of the Neighborhood Youth Council ◀

- To provide student representation throughout the Neighborhood & Family Life Program to openly discuss matters of student interest and concern
- To create an awareness of the importance of the student home and surrogate family
- To emphasize acceptance of individual and group responsibility as the basis for personal success, neighborhood improvement, and student achievement
- To suggest ways of enhancing life within the student home, the neighborhood, and the school community; to seek solutions to challenges; and

to promote worthwhile programs, activities, and service projects
- To establish open communication and positive relationships between the students and all with whom they may come in contact, directly or indirectly
- To develop leadership in the elected Neighborhood Youth Council and promote good citizenship in the student body through awareness of, and involvement in, the processes and responsibilities of student governance
- To foster unity and good morale among the students

▶ *The Responsibilities of the Neighborhood Youth Council* ◀
in conjunction with the advisers:

- To represent the feelings and wishes of the students in their neighborhood in all discussions and decisions concerning them. All resulting statements or decisions will be considered by the neighborhood administration as the official voice of the students within that neighborhood
- To present to the neighborhood administration recommendations (suggestions for action), resolutions (statements of the feelings of the students), and reports (for informational purposes)
- To communicate directly with the students in their neighborhood for the purpose of Neighborhood Youth Council business

- To initiate and carry out projects for itself or the student body
- To engage in correspondence, commendations, and the other usual activities of the deliberating representative group
- To establish regulations concerning its own members relative to attendance at meetings, behavior at meetings, and membership
- To function in any other capacity or to assume any other authority granted by the neighborhood administration either on a temporary or permanent basis

THE ORION PROGRAM

Dan Fey, school-to-work coordinator at Kalispell High School, in Kalispell, Montana, began the Orion Program in 1999. He selected community leaders—the county sheriff, business leaders, retired military officers, housewives, U.S. Senator field representatives—and asked them to become mentors to high school students at risk for dropping out of school. The students aren't compelled to enter the program, but virtually all have been glad to do it.

One student was linked up with the county sheriff, who was described to the student as someone who dropped out of high school, got his degree in the navy, and then became the county sheriff. The student later told a teacher that although he didn't think he'd need to see his mentor much, he was really impressed that the sheriff gave him his phone number and said that he could call at any time. The student later dropped out, but eventually returned to the school, saying that he'd gone to the Job Corps, earned his G.E.D., and gotten a job. The student appeared more focused, more confident, and more motivated.

Ingredients

One community mentor for each student in the program
Two counselors to select students
One coordinator to select and train mentors

Instructions

1 Select community leaders and invite them to become mentors.

2 Have counselors select high school students who have poor attendance or grades or who are otherwise at risk for dropping out.

3 Give the mentors a 90-minute training session and then pair them with the students at the high school.

4 Have mentors commit to maintaining contact with the students at least once a month, the contact consisting of anything from going to a movie to talking on the phone to meeting over coffee to exchanging cards. (Be sure to check your school's or district's guidelines for issues of safety and liability.)

Chef

Dan Fey, *school-to-work coordinator,* Flathead High School, 644 4th Avenue, Kalispell, MT 59901, 406-751-3503, feyd@sd5.k12.mt.us, www.sd5.k12.mt.us

Nutrients

#3—Other adult relationships, #4—Caring neighborhood, #21—Achievement motivation

Serves

Up to 100 students, grades 10–12

Variations

▶ You can make the mentoring schedule more structured, for example, by stipulating the number of meetings or activities. Some of these meetings could be at school; others might take place away from school.

▶ You can have a "shadow day," when the mentor follows the student throughout a typical school day to get an idea of what the student's day is like.

▶ *Suggested Mentor Activities* ◀

What you are not.	Your role as a mentor is to be an additional adult resource in a student's life while at FHS. *You are not expected to be a truant officer, psychologist, money lender, surrogate parent, innkeeper, or teacher.*
Things you can do with a student.	• Maintain current phone number and address. • Maintain contact frequently with your student, at least once a month. • Meet at FHS, coffee shop, business location; send a fax or e-mail. • Send a postcard on a monthly basis. • Send a birthday card. • Send a congratulatory card when your student achieves an objective or goal. • Visit your student's classroom (recommend the first three class periods). • Attend sporting or extracurricular events. • Take your student to lunch. • Encourage your student to join a club or try out for a sport. • *Encourage the student to stay in school, earn a diploma, and call you for assistance.*
What Is an At-Risk Student?	• Students with a higher chance of dropping out of school. Encourage them to stay in school and graduate. • They drop out because of a meaningless school experience, feelings of inadequacy, fear of failure, economic factors, feelings of being ignored. • They have to work, take care of a family crisis, or feel they cannot recover from low grades. • They are disconnected from school activities, their peers, and adults. Family and support networks may be lacking. • They reinforce negative thoughts about themselves. Help them to think positive. • They lack social skills. They desire secure relationships and want to belong. • They wish to be in charge of themselves, but have not been taught basic decision-making and leadership skills. Offer advice, but let them make the right choices. • If they lack support for school/education, provide that support for them.

★ THE SCHOOL OF CLUBS

No one's left out in the 7th and 8th grades of Brandon, Mississippi's Northwest Rankin Middle School; that's because *every* student is a member of a club and *every* teacher coordinates a club. Students do everything from working on nature trails to designing Web pages to building a courtyard to inviting guest speakers on a variety of topics; virtually all the activities are fun, largely because the students themselves choose the activities. Getting good grades means they can go off campus. In any event, the students determine which clubs exist and which clubs they join. Students rule in this school; and they all belong.

Ingredients

Informal surveys
Coordination of clubs for 30 minutes a week
Adult advisers
Resources to do service projects

Instructions

1 In the spring, survey students to determine what kinds of school clubs they'd like to belong to; be sure to survey incoming students from other schools, too.

2 Compile a list of clubs, distribute it to students, and ask them to make first, second, and third choices.

3 Give all students their first choice unless too few students (say, fewer than 25) sign up for a club; then give those students their second choice.

4 Let school adults sign up to coordinate each club; assign the remainder.

5 In the fall, let students know which club they'll be participating in for the rest of the year.

6 Convene the clubs for 30 minutes once a week.

7 Be sure that every club decides on and follows through with a service project each semester.

Chef

Kathy Jones, *counselor,* Northwest Rankin Middle School, One Paw Print Place, Brandon, MS 39047, 601-992-4110, kjones@rcsd.k12.ms.us

Nutrients

#18—Youth programs, #17—Creative activities, #24—Bonding to school

Serves

700 students, grades 7–8

Variations

▶ You can alter a variety of the details in this activity—the amount of time students spend in their clubs, the number of times you reconfigure clubs, the number of clubs, and the number of service projects.
▶ You can set up clubs for school adults, too.

EXTRA HELPINGS for *The School of Clubs: A list of service projects initiated by student clubs.*

▶ Northwest Rankin Middle School Service Projects ◀
by Club, Spring Semester 2000

- **Collectibles Club**—provided a snack tray for patients and families at Ronald McDonald House
- **Computer Club**—cleaned the two computer discovery labs
- **Cooking Club**—collected and donated nonperishables to Gateway Mission
- **Drama Club**—read to 2nd-grade classes at NWR Elementary for 30 minutes and gave them a bookmark to encourage the joy of reading; conducted a schoolwide initiative to bring items for the Jackson Animal Rescue League
- **Fashion Club**—donated clothes to the Salvation Army
- **Future Educators of America**—made pop-up books for the children's center connected with Shoe String Operation and Wells Memorial United Methodist Church
- **Golf Club**—planted dogwood trees and five other hardwood trees during National Tree Planting Week at the school
- **Grands**—visited Lakeland Nursing Home, Crossgates Nursing Home, and Heritage House to spend time with residents, deliver Easter cards, and decorate eggs with happy quotes inside; planted flowers at Heritage House
- **Hunting and Fishing Club**—identified tracks of various wildlife around the school Nature Trail; built rustic signs showing a picture of the animal and its tracks
- **Music Club**—collected money for Easter Seals
- **Spirit Club and Taebo Club**—honored the girls' and boys' basketball teams with a reception
- **Strategy Games Club**—brought caps and hats to give to cancer patients; with Footprints, held benefit concert for Baptist Children's Village
- **Techno-Millennium Club**—made Easter treat bags for teachers

STEPPIN' UP TO SOLUTIONS

This program started about five years ago as a way to help young people submit better grant proposals. In upstate New York, the City/County Youth Council, 20 students from high schools around the county, was in charge of awarding grants to groups of young people who wanted to do things to improve their community. They decided to draw up an outline that helped young people not only write better proposals but also better assess what needed to be done in their communities. The outline has been improved over the years, until now the program encompasses process and product. The process is two conferences, each of which attracts more than 150 people, as well as other workshops and forms of technical assistance. The product is an interactive planning guide—*Steppin' Up to Solutions,* available from the chef—that young people use to help them plan community projects.

Ingredients

Space for conferences
Conference facilitators
Advertising

Instructions

1 Schedule an all-day conference at a high school on a Saturday in November; invite young people interested generally in planning community projects and particularly in applying to the local source of national Youth as Resources grants. Establish the criterion that participants come in groups of 7–10, accompanied by an adult adviser.

2 Advertise the conference through schools, newspapers, and other media.

3 At the conference, help participants:
▶ Learn how to better assess the needs of their community;
▶ Learn how to better assess the strengths and resources of their community; and

▶ Learn how to match the needs, the resources, and their abilities in order to plan a project or service that improves the community.

4 Immediately after the conference, help each group prepare for their project by reviewing their plans, suggesting improvements, referring them to resources, and so on.

5 Hold a second conference in February—not only for groups who have been awarded grants but for other groups who may be implementing projects as well. At this conference, focus on team building, sharing ideas, celebrating successes, and improving outcomes. Conclude this conference with a dance.

Chef

LaWanda Shipman, Youth Participation Project, Rochester/Monroe County Youth Bureau, 4160 City-Place, 50 West Main Street, Rochester, NY 14614, 716-428-4929

Nutrients

#8—Youth as resources, #32—Planning and decision making, #37—Personal power

Serves

150 young people, ages 10–18

Variations

▶ Instead of one large conference, you can have smaller conferences that focus on, for example, younger or older adolescents, smaller or larger projects, and more specific needs.
▶ You can bring in participants from previous years' conferences to share what they've learned.

► *Steppin' Up to Solutions* ◄
by Malik Evans

Strengthening our communities
Taking time to show we care
Expressing ourselves in a civil manner
Pushing forward for the implementation of positive projects
Pulling in resources we may not yet have
Igniting energy that is contagious
Naming our needs so they can be met

Undermining the negative vibes we may get from negative forces
Paying special attention to those who need assistance

Trying our hardest to push successful implementation
Opening the eyes of those in our communities

Striving for excellence
Operating efficient projects
Looping together our ideas in one
Uniting different communities
Taking time to show we care
Issuing actions of change
Opening DOORS TO EVERYONE
Naming #1 PRIORITIES
Saving OUR FUTURE

**Some of the activities
in the guide:**

- Brainstorming "rules of respect" you'll follow for the rest of the process

- Reviewing the five community outcomes that were created for Rochester, New York, and discussing which outcomes may fit your area

- Describing your community

- Distinguishing between what your community has and what it needs

- Identifying developmental assets that you could start doing today

- Selecting community outcomes to work on

- Brainstorming the steps to take to create a project that will accomplish the goal

- Planning the project

- Fashioning the project statement

- Creating a project logo

- Developing a timeline

STRENGTHS IN FAMILIES

Patchworks is an initiative growing out of the PATCH (Planned Approach To Community Health) process. In its third year, the initiative is cochaired by Diane Gubatayao and a student. For years, budget restraints prevented Alaska's Ketchikan-Gateway Borough School District from having social workers in schools. But two things happened: One was a state reallocation of funds, and the other was a community forum at which parents voiced strong support for having social workers in schools. Now, though the funding is still tenuous (it's currently funded with Drug-Free Schools money), two social workers serve six elementary and middle schools. They use the asset model: Because already-troubled families are further stressed and defensive when confronted with their children's problems, the school social workers address the families' strengths. The response from the beginning has been very positive.

One example of how the asset framework can be effective in situations like these was a 13-year-old girl whose single mother had four other children. The girl wasn't doing well in school. One of the school social workers, Bett Jabuvek, discovered that the girl really wanted to go to college and become an artist. Jabuvek found mentors for her at the middle school and helped her find time to be with the art teacher. She even set her up in an art class. This was the toehold that Jabuvek needed to be able to talk with the girl's family. By focusing on the girl's strengths, as well as the desire of the mother to do what was best for her daughter, Jabuvek was able to address the situation.

Ingredients

> School social workers
>
> Access to families

Instructions

1 Identify situations in which a teacher can't make headway with the parents of a child who is having problems, for example, poor attendance or "acting out."

2 Meet with the parents for about 45 minutes, either at the parents' home or another place outside school.

3 Get a sense of the family's strengths and base suggestions on those strengths (e.g., "Well, you can't be home for dinner with your child, but do you sit down as a family for breakfast?"). Use asset language when it's appropriate.

4 Have parents recall their own teenage years to get them to think about what they might have needed as children.

Chefs

Diane Gubatayao, Patchworks, 3054 Fifth Avenue, Ketchikan, AK 99901, 907-225-4350; **Bett Jabuvek and Mary Alexander,** *school social workers,* Ketchikan-Gateway Borough School District, 333 Schoenbar Road, Ketchikan, AK 99901, 907-225-2118

Nutrients

#6—Parent involvement in schooling, #5—Caring school climate, #11—Family boundaries

Serves

Families of students, grades K–8

Variations

▶ All school adults—counselors, teachers, nurses, administrators, support staff, coaches, bus drivers—can use the approach of focusing on students' strengths rather than their problems.

▶ You can also use the approach of occasionally meeting parents on their own turf—or on neutral turf—rather than at school, which can be threatening to some parents, especially those with a history of bad school experiences.

STUDENT-LED CONFERENCES

It's such a basic idea, and it goes right to the core of students taking on responsibility. In rural Gillette, Wyoming—specifically, in Pronghorn Elementary School—students in grades 3–6 and some in grade 2 lead conferences with their teachers and parents. Marianne Baysinger, who teaches 3rd-grade students this year, says that she's even done it with 1st-grade students. The students set the agenda, they talk about what they've learned and what they hope to learn, and they tell their parents who they consider the most important people in their lives.

"They learn that school is important," says Baysinger, "that it's their job, and they're accountable for it." They also gain focus by reflecting on the topics of the conference, they gain confidence from leading the conference, and they gain an opportunity to talk simultaneously to their teacher and parents about their life at school.

Ingredients

Times and place for parent-teacher-student conferences
Older student volunteers to practice with younger
students

Instructions

1 About two weeks before parent-teacher conferences, ask students to begin thinking about what they've learned in school the previous several months and to write about the following:

▶ What they've learned in the various subject areas, for example, math, reading, writing, and science;

▶ What they've noticed that was particularly interesting;

▶ What they need to work on;

▶ What behavioral goals they might have (e.g., to be more courteous or to be more focused); and

▶ Who they think are the most important people in their life, and why.

Allow about 15 minutes a day for students to do this, and keep all their work in individual folders.

2 Also during this time, tell students that they'll be leading the upcoming parent-teacher conference. Give them a summary of the agenda of the conference, which in large part will follow what they've written in their folders.

3 Give students at least two opportunities to practice leading the conference, for example, with older students.

4 When you set up the conference, let parents know that their children will be leading it, and ask them not to bring siblings.

5 When you hold the conferences, allow the students to lead the discussion about what they've learned, what they thought was particularly interesting, what they need to work on, what behavioral goals they hope to achieve, and who they think are the most important people in their lives, and why (have them read this aloud). At the end of the conference, have students ask you and the parent(s) whether you want to talk about anything in their absence; the students can then wait in the hallway if you wish to talk.

Chef

Marianne Baysinger, *teacher,* Pronghorn Elementary School, 3005 Oakcrest, Gillette, WY 82718, 307-682-1676

Nutrients

#6—Parent involvement in schooling, #21—Achievement motivation, #30—Responsibility

Serves

300 students, grades 2–6

Variations

▶ You can do this activity at any grade level, varying the amount of support you give the student on the basis of the student's ability.

▶ You can incorporate other items into the agenda for the conference, again, on the basis of the age and ability of the student, for example, a self-report on which developmental assets students feel they have and which they feel they need, a plan for the rest of the year, long-term goals, and suggestions for the classroom and school.

 EXTRA HELPINGS for *Student-Led Conferences: A form to help students prepare to lead a conference with their parents and teacher.*

▶ *Reflecting on Myself* ◀

Name _____ Grade _____

At the beginning, middle, and end of the year, rate yourself on the following items.

	Date_____	Date_____	Date_____
I AM RESPONSIBLE.			
I do all the work I'm asked to do.			
I ask for help when I need it.			
I check to see that my work is my best.			
I turn my work in on time.			
I AM MOTIVATED.			
I think learning is important.			
I want to learn.			
I am doing all I am able to do.			
I care about doing my best.			
I AM SELF-CONFIDENT.			
I believe I can learn.			
I know mistakes are part of learning.			
I learn from my mistakes.			
I can learn even if the work is hard.			
I GET ALONG WITH MY CLASSMATES.			
I am helpful and friendly.			
I listen to others' ideas.			
I share and take turns.			
I don't use put-downs.			
I talk about problems with my friends.			

HOW CAN I IMPROVE MY WORK?

_____

★ UPSTAIRS

In 1997, the *Search Institute Profiles of Student Life: Attitudes and Behaviors* self-report survey—developed by Search Institute expressly to measure the extent to which students in grades 6–12 have the 40 developmental assets—was given to students in grades 7–12 in Hazen, North Dakota. From the results of that survey came an eight-hour meeting with 60 adults and 20 teenagers. And from that meeting came a leadership team that continues to set goals and strategies each year. The team brainstormed how to find a place for "kids to hang out," a significant need for young people in Hazen. After an article in the local newspaper, phone calls about possibilities, small-town word of mouth, and one or two false starts, they checked into an unused hockey arena—about 4,000 square feet—and wrote a proposal. The hockey group listened to the proposal and decided to invest in the town's youth; they donated the rent for the space.

The result was Upstairs, so called because it's upstairs at the hockey arena. It has pool tables, arcade games, a quiet room, couches, and VCRs. It's open on Friday and Saturday nights, 8:30 till midnight. An adult volunteer from the faith community staffs it. Concessions are sold, but there's no admission fee. About 25–30 young people show up on an average weekend. Maxine Beckwith, counselor at Hazen High School, watched two girls sit there for a couple of hours, just talking. "It's just so fun to sit here," they said. "Everyone is nonjudgmental. We're safe." Beckwith says that "whatever you do, you need kids involved," but reminds others that "you don't accomplish this overnight. Change is slow."

Ingredients

Money to acquire (e.g., by lease) space and furnish it with games and equipment used by teenagers
Contributions from families and businesses
Volunteers to staff and manage the facility

Instructions

1 Acquire a building that is no longer being used. Ask property management companies, city officials, and so on, sharing your plans for the space.

2 Solicit contributions from families and businesses, for example:
▶ Wiring the building or installing plumbing
▶ Staffing
▶ Offering discounts on materials like wood and sheetrock
▶ Creating and providing artwork

3 Furnish the space with pool tables, Ping-Pong tables, arcade games, a television, a stereo system, a VCR, a "quiet room," and couches and chairs.

4 Furnish the kitchen with a refrigerator, freezer, pizza oven, and sink.

5 Sell concessions, but charge no admission fee.

6 Open the facility at appropriate times, for example, from 8:30 to midnight Friday and Saturday evenings, from late August to late April.

7 Solicit the cooperation of faith communities and youth-serving organizations to supply chaperones, rotating responsibilities every month.

8 Have a youth board coordinate the facility; the board can include about 15 students from grades 9–12 and meet weekly, if possible.

Chef

Maxine Beckwith, *counselor,* Hazen High School, 502 1st Avenue NE, Hazen, ND 58545, 701-748-2345, beckwitm@hazen.k12.nd.us

Nutrients

#10—Safety, #30—Responsibility, #37—Personal power

Serves

25–30 students/weekend, grades 9–12

Variations

▶ If funds or issues of accessibility are a problem, you may be able to rent rooms in buildings—or get them donated by social service organizations—to meet your needs.

▶ You can solicit families—parents and children—to act as weekly "hosts" for the space.

 EXTRA HELPINGS for *Upstairs: The Upstairs Story.*

▶ *The Upstairs Story* ◀
by Upstairs manager Teri Finneman

We started thinking of the idea for Upstairs in the spring of 1999. Lee's, the former teen hangout, had just closed down, and the only thing for teenagers to do in a town of 3,000 was to cruise Main for four hours every night.

In March/April the first meetings of the Youth Board were held. At our first meeting, we elected officers: two cochairs, secretary, treasurer, and public relations officers. We discussed the issue of rules at length. What rules could we come up with that would keep our place running, yet not scare people away by being too strict in a place for kids?

We decided on these rules:

- No smoking inside the building.
- A youth board member and one adult chaperone would be on hand from 8:30 to midnight every Friday and Saturday evening.
- "Respect yourself, others, and Upstairs."
- Our age range was freshmen and up. (We decided against an upper age limit due to the fact that we did not think it would be an issue.)

These rules have worked great for us. . . .

Now that we had our idea in mind, we had to find a place that would be big enough for teenagers, have a good location, and hopefully not be a financial burden. Our original hopes had been to have the teen center on Main Street, like Lee's had been. This is where the kids are. However, after looking into a few options, we realized the All Seasons hockey arena was going to be our best bet. It was out of the way from close neighbors, there was plenty of parking, the space was huge, and best of all, it was free of rent.

Once we had our big unfinished area, the work began. We spent the summer of '99 sheetrocking, painting, building a wall to separate the area into the main room and a quiet room, ordering supplies such as food, fund-raising, and finding equipment and furniture. Many, many hours were put into beginning this project.

As we began to work, many adults and kids doubted us. When I tried to find pool tables and arcade games, I was turned down because "teen centers don't last." Finally, we did find a supplier. . . . it is uncountable how many comments were made on how it would never work, no one would go, and we couldn't do it. But we didn't care. We were doing it and it was going to work. It's funny when I think about it now. My friend, Beth (cochair), and I . . . had wanted to be open when school got out in May. Our next deadline goal was early June. Then it was July. Finally, on August 21 . . . Upstairs opened for business.

⬛ VOCATIONS ON-SITE

Howard High School of Technology is a vocational school of about 800 students located in downtown Wilmington, Delaware. What makes the school noteworthy is not just that its instructors teach their students useful skills and trades; it's also that they provide their students with many ways to use those skills and trades to serve their community. Principal Joyce Ayres says that 73 percent of her students do some kind of service-learning, that is, do something for the community related to their specialty. This particular focus has led to a relationship with nearby Windsor House, a high-rise apartment facility for low-income senior citizens. Students have been there twice already, and Ayres has plans for similar activities during the year.

These activities benefit all involved: the senior citizens, who not only receive services and companionship but also, as Ayres says, "feel better about teenagers" in general as a result; and the students, who have the opportunity to see tangible—and not so tangible—results of their work and, presumably, their choice of vocation. Ayres sums up the involvement like this: "If both groups feel better and more comfortable about the other, the day and the continued work are priceless."

Ingredients

Coordination with the target population
Supplies related to vocational areas

Instructions

1 Set up a liaison with a nearby home for the elderly.

2 Plan a day—or part of a day—in which students can use what they've learned to serve the senior citizens, for example:

▶ Students in cosmetology giving manicures and pedicures
▶ Students in culinary arts providing soup and sandwiches

▶ Students in nursing technology offering blood pressure screenings and basic medical information
▶ Students in dental assistance offering dental and denture care, and giving out dental and denture supplies
▶ Students in public services presenting a video on fraud and safety tips

3 Invite any student who wants to participate, including, for example, cheerleaders to conduct instructional, low-impact, aerobic exercises, and other students to talk, play cards, serve refreshments, and generally be companions to the senior citizens.

4 Coordinate with the parent/teacher/student association for transportation, preparation, and other volunteer duties.

5 Set up different areas at the facility to provide all the services.

6 Take photographs of the event, and plan similar activities throughout the year.

Chef

Joyce Ayres, *principal,* Howard High School of Technology, 401 East 12th Street, Wilmington, DE 19801, 302-571-5400; joyce@nccvt.k12.de.us

Nutrients

#39—Sense of purpose, #26—Caring, #40—Positive view of personal future

Serves

50–60 students, grades 9–12

Variations

▶ Obviously, a vocational school has an advantage over other schools in the services they provide, but most schools can do some of the things that Howard High School of Technology does. You can canvass your students to identify what they can offer and match it to what the target population needs. For younger grades, you can first identify the population and the need, after which you can train the students to provide that need.

▶ To deepen the experience for students, plan a reflective activity after each service activity, to include such components as group discussion of what was learned and observed, the keeping of a student service journal, or the creation of a notebook that includes stories, reports, and pictures.

Side Dishes

SIDE DISHES may be programs that affect only a small portion of the school community, or they may be activities of short duration. The advantage of implementing side dishes is that they can be a first step toward more substantial asset-building programs but without the risk of involving high numbers of staff and students.

▶ *The Recipes* ◀

After-School Homework Clubs *(Idaho)*

Anger Management? *(Washington)*

Artists in Classrooms *(Utah)*

ASK *(Idaho)*

Bridge *(Virginia)*

Business Links *(Texas)*

CLUE *(Georgia)*

Foster Grandparents *(Kansas)*

The HERO Program *(Washington)*

Kids as Shoppers *(Washington)*

Kids in the Hall *(Kansas)*

Kindness Chains *(Washington)*

Learn to Earn *(Florida)*

Learning to Volunteer *(Colorado)*

Lunch Buddies *(South Carolina)*

Math Buddies *(New Hampshire)*

Ministry to Neighborhood Children *(Louisiana)*

The Proud Panther (Arkansas)

The Race, Culture, and Ethnicity Workshop *(Massachusetts)*

READ *(Oklahoma)*

Save One Student *(North Carolina)*

School-Grown Vegetables *(Hawaii)*

The School on Wheels *(Ohio)*

Seniors on the Internet *(Iowa)*

Share a Friend *(Illinois)*

A 6th-Grade Yarn *(Maine)*

Students Who Care *(Wisconsin)*

The Sunshine Club *(Rhode Island)*

Teen Pages (Minnesota)

X-TEND *(Michigan)*

AFTER-SCHOOL HOMEWORK CLUBS

Nampa, Idaho's after-school homework clubs began in about 1995 when schoolteachers got together and decided that they wanted to do something more for students— many of them from low-income, single-parent families— who needed just a little more support to succeed in school; they call these students "kids on the edge." The first club served students in elementary school; now there are several more, at least one of them in middle school. The clubs are distinct from one another; local control dictates the precise nature of each club.

Aside from the students' doing better in school, parents report that their evenings are much more pleasant now because their children are more at ease. Another benefit is that before participating in the homework clubs, many students from single-parent families had spent their afternoons alone in front of a television; since participating in the clubs, they've gained companionship as well as support.

One teacher drove the major benefit home with a single question. Speaking before her fellow teachers, she asked if anyone had ever woken up in the morning and realized they were unprepared for that day's responsibilities. She said that anxiety is what some children feel every day— the fear of being called on, the sense that they somehow failed. The homework clubs help allay those feelings.

Ingredients

Adult volunteers
An adult coordinator
A place to meet

Instructions

1 Have teachers identify students who want or need more support for succeeding in school.

2 Contact students' families, inviting the students to an "after-school homework club"; encourage students to sign a contract agreeing to participate.

3 Secure places to meet outside school but in students' neighborhoods, for example, a basement in a church or temple, the Housing Authority, a charity such as the Salvation Army, or rooms used by youth-serving organizations such as Boys and Girls Clubs.

4 Have adult volunteers meet with students about two afternoons a week after school for about two hours. Set an agenda similar to the following:
▶ Have a snack;
▶ Review homework from the past day or two;
▶ Do current homework; and
▶ Plan for tests or other homework in the next day or two.

5 Participate in occasional events like field trips to make the homework club more enjoyable.

6 Establish liaisons with students' teachers to monitor progress and adapt focus.

Chef

Lynn Borud, Healthy Nampa Healthy Youth, Mercy Medical Center, 1512 12th Avenue Road, Nampa, ID 83686, 208-463-5870

Nutrients

#23—Homework, #3—Other adult relationships, #21—Achievement motivation

Serves

100 students, grades 4–8

Variations

▶ Use cross-age teaching for middle school homework clubs; that is, ask high school students to volunteer.
▶ Use peer tutoring by pairing up students in the clubs for part of the time or by inviting other middle school students to volunteer as tutors.

♥ ANGER MANAGEMENT?

The Denny Wellness Center is a clinic in a Seattle public middle school of about 850 students, consisting of two counselors and a nurse-practitioner who works in conjunction with the school nurse; this is the third year of the clinic's operation. Previously, students who exhibited a pattern of misbehavior and anger would be referred to the clinic by teachers because they needed a place for "anger management." Mental health counselor Laurie Van Diest, however, became disillusioned with the negativity and felt that she first had to convince the students that they weren't "bad." That's when she changed philosophies from "anger management" to "asset development."

"We may think we know what their issues are, but they need to do it in their own way in their own time," says Van Diest. For example, it turned out that the boys' group became a grief group, because what they all had in common was the loss of a primary female caretaker. Since the advent of the new philosophy, problems have decreased, and test scores are up.

Van Diest is optimistic about the change, and she's pushing on ahead, starting an after-school asset team of 30 fired-up students. "This is a good fit for me," she says. "It's where I live and breathe."

Ingredients

Trained counselors
Locations for group work

Instructions

1 Working with students who have been referred as "management problems," get permissions from parents and from students to enroll the students in groups to discuss their issues.

2 Assemble groups of six to nine students, segregated by sex.

3 Meet with them for one class period a week; rotate the classes students will miss.

4 Focus discussions on students' issues and strengths rather than their "deficiencies."

5 Establish and reinforce adult relationships with the students, and then encourage teachers and other school adults to do the same. Discourage the idea of trying to "fix" the students.

6 Revamp forms to reflect the asset philosophy. For example, change a Student Stress Scale to a Student Strength Scale.

Chef

Laurie Van Diest, *mental health counselor,* Denny Wellness Center, Denny Middle School, 8402 30th Avenue SW, Seattle, WA 98126, 206-923-2809

Nutrients

#36—Peaceful conflict resolution, #29—Honesty, #30—Responsibility

Serves

Groups of six to nine students, grades 6–8

Variations

▶ You can review all forms relating to student behavior and amend them to focus on the asset framework, for example, their strengths and the positive relationships they can make and sustain.

▶ You can talk to parents about reframing their perspective away from fixing problems and toward encouraging strengths, for their children and for themselves.

ARTISTS IN CLASSROOMS

Elementary school principal Sally Sanders secured a grant for two types of art education to occur simultaneously—one for teachers (a state specialist) and the other for students in 22 classrooms (a visual artist). The effect was that students became interested in drawing, painting, and other forms of art, and teachers felt more confident teaching them. One teacher said, "In 22 years, I've been afraid to teach art. But today I drew the most wonderful stegosaurus on the chalkboard—in front of the class!"

When teachers are placed in the role of students, and when those teachers can relate their experiences to their own students, they set themselves up as great role models. Their students get the powerful messages that learning is not only for young people, that learning is sometimes difficult, and that learning is often extremely rewarding.

Ingredients

An art educator
An artist
Access to teachers

Instructions

1 Provide three or four monthly 2½-hour in-services for teachers on art, art history, and teaching art topics.

2 At the same time, have visual artists visit each classroom once or twice a week—discussing art, demonstrating different forms of artistic expression, and promoting creativity through art.

3 Incorporate art into subsequent curricula.

Chef

Sally Sanders, *principal,* Jackling Elementary School, 3760 South 4610 West, West Valley City, UT 84120, 801-964-7515

Nutrients

#17—Creative activities, #14—Adult role models, #21—Achievement motivation

Serves

620 students, grades K–6

Variations

▶ You can use the same two-pronged approach (teachers and students getting information simultaneously) in a variety of topics—health, science, music, and so on.

▶ You can focus on art from different cultures, thus imparting even more information that's relevant to the particular school population.

ASK

ASK stands for Ask Seniors who Know, now in its fifth year. Because the peer-helping group is planned and run by 12th-grade students, and because new students come in each year, the activities may differ from year to year. The focus is usually on positive activities—things that students can do in the school and their community that are fun but that also keep them safe and healthy. ASK also provides opportunities for students to talk over issues with other students when they may not want to do so with adults. The group is evidently very empowering. As Debbie Hastings, one of the advisers to the program, says about the students, "They call the shots."

Ingredients

Access to assemblies
Information about peer helping

Instructions

1 Initially, choose a diverse group of 10 students, grade 12, who are self-motivated, communicative, and trusted by their peers (ask for nominations from all students and school adults).

2 Hold weekly meetings to discuss how to promote safe and healthy choices.

3 Pursue a variety of activities, for example:
▶ Working with local junior high schools to put on assemblies about healthy choices in regard to drugs, sex, and violence
▶ Putting on assemblies for incoming sophomores and outgoing seniors

▶ Organizing "Club Fairs" to give students an idea of the variety of clubs in the school
▶ Making the ASK students available to students who have questions about school or who want to talk over issues

4 Have the outgoing ASK students help choose the new ASK students.

Chefs

Kali Krudy, *teacher,* and **Debbie Hastings,** *nurse,* Borah High School, 6001 Cassia, Boise, ID 83709, 208-322-3855

Nutrients

#31—Restraint, #15—Positive peer influence, #35—Resistance skills

Serves

1,800 students, grades 10–12

Variations

▶ You can choose a team of students from each grade level (thus, "Ask *Students* who Know").
▶ You can organize meetings between each ASK student and her or his "constituency," that is, any students who want to give their "representative" feedback or suggestions.

♥ BRIDGE

Gail Lentz's official title is "administrative aide," but over the past couple of decades she has a found a multitude of ways to both administer and give aid. For the past 13 years she has worked with the Bridge program, a kind of omnibus mentoring program whose tenet is that a good relationship between a student and a caring school adult is the basis for school success.

And success is definitely the key word for this program. Lentz focuses on the students who are at risk of not graduating with their class, for whatever reason, but often because of distractions in their home life or because of health problems. She coordinates anywhere from 60 to 100 students, as well as about 40–60 school adults—teachers, administrators, support staff, and administrative staff. At times she has had to be imaginative in matching students with staff: The only interest of one girl, who had cystic fibrosis, seemed to be mashed potatoes, which the girl loved. So Lentz matched her with one of the cafeteria workers, who made sure to give the girl extra mashed potatoes whenever it was on the menu.

Lentz has been around long enough to see former Bridge students—some of whom didn't graduate with their class but who later got a G.E.D.—return and personally thank their mentors. But by far the biggest thrill, she says, comes on that day when the students walk across the stage to get their diplomas.

Ingredients

Coordination of school adults with students

Instructions

1 Identify students who are at risk of not graduating with their class. Solicit self-referrals as well as referrals from recent middle school counselors, current high school counselors, teachers, parents, siblings, and so on.

2 Send out a questionnaire to all school adults about their hobbies, their interests, and their willingness to be part of a program in which they act as mentor to a student.

3 Follow up the questionnaire by meeting with the interested students to find out, for example, whether they have any favorite teachers or other school adults, and by meeting with adults to focus on the logistics of the program.

4 Match up all the students who want to be part of the program with the school adults, based on common interests and previous relationships.

5 Set up a system by which the adults will continually encourage students, provide them with access to cocurricular activities, work with them on improving their grades (students could give the mentors copies of their grades), and give them the support they need to graduate.

Chef

Gail Lentz, *coordinator,* Bridge program, Menchville High School, 275 Menchville Road, Newport News, VA 23602, 757-886-7722

Nutrients

#21—Achievement motivation, #3—Other adult relationships, #5—Caring school climate

Serves

Up to 100 students, grades 9–12

Variations

▶ You can coordinate a program like Bridge in lower grade levels; at any level, you can organize a celebratory party at the end of the year for all graduating Bridge students and their mentors.

▶ You can invite students to share what *they* are experts in and to teach that to interested teachers and other school adults.

 EXTRA HELPINGS for *Bridge: A memo to school staff.*

▶ *Memo* ◀

Our school dropout prevention program, Bridge, has been one of Menchville High School's most successful programs. We have made the difference in hundreds of at-risk lives. Our program has been nationally recognized and cited as a best practice by the Southern Association of Colleges and Schools and High Schools That Work.

Our faculty and staff have been the driving force with their time and support. Please join us by volunteering to mentor a student.

Please complete the form below and return to Gail Lentz in room 116.

PROGRAM OBJECTIVES

1. Create an "at-school" friendship with the student. Be someone who will notice when the student is absent and care enough to find out why.
2. Establish a rapport with the student so that the student can talk to you about goals, concerns, and feelings.
3. Check behind the student to see that the student is attending school and classes regularly and punctually.
4. Check to see that the student is meeting academic responsibilities.
5. Provide encouragement and "pep talks" when appropriate.
6. Help the student set and achieve goals. Be the student's advocate.

PLEASE FILL IN AND RETURN:

1. Your name and Professional Planning Period _____

2. Have you ever been a Bridge mentor? _____

3. Would you prefer to mentor a particular student? If yes, fill in the name. _____

4. Would you prefer to mentor a _____ male or _____ female student? What age or grade level? _____

5. Would you consent to tutoring a student in your subject area or another? _____

   If yes, what subject? _____

6. What hobbies or sports do you enjoy? _____

7. What are your expectations of the program? _____

   _____

8. What questions do you need answered concerning this program? _____

   _____

   _____

🍎 BUSINESS LINKS

Georgetown, Texas, has a population of about 25,000, and Benold Middle School and Tippit Middle School have run this semester-long program since 1996; it has involved about 300 8th-grade students from each school. The program has two purposes: to acquaint students with different careers, and to show them how relevant their schooling is.

Sometimes those purposes are achieved serendipitously: On a visit to an assembly line, one student, not academically inclined, got bored and complained to his teacher that it was meaningless, tedious work. She told him that unless he improved his grades, this was the kind of job in which he might be destined to spend most of the rest of his life. For the first time, said the teacher, a light seemed to go on in the young man's head.

On another occasion, an employee at a manufacturing plant saw the students coming down the hall and stopped them to relate how he had dropped out and how much he thought he should have stayed in school. "School is so important," he told them, and students said later that of all the things they saw and heard that day, what the man said had the most impact on them.

Ingredients

> Liaisons with local businesses
> Permission to take students from school for a day
> Transportation to and from businesses

Instructions

1 Identify and analyze students' career interests with a formal measure like the Differential Aptitude Test (for information about the measure, write Harcourt Brace Educational Measurement, 555 Academic Court, San Antonio, TX 78204) or with less formal interest inventories.

2 Link local individuals and businesses (e.g., manufacturing plants, physicians, attorneys, merchants) with students.

3 On a predetermined day, bring three or four students—along with a parent, teacher, or other school representative—to a business, and there have the businessperson show the students what that business is like; for example:

▶ The owner of a small sign company showed students how to draw signs, and in particular how to use math and algebra to do it.

▶ The owner of a manufacturing company talked about the future in terms of his company and then took everyone to lunch.

Make the experience as hands-on as possible, and try to build the connections between what students are learning at school and their career options after they graduate.

Chef

Rhonda Farney, *executive director,* Georgetown Partners in Education, 2211 North Austin Avenue, Georgetown, TX 78626, 512-943-5137

Nutrients

#21—Achievement motivation, #32—Planning and decision making, #40—Positive view of personal future

Serves

600 students, grade 8

Variations

▶ You can make connections with the PTA so that students' parents can act as the businesspeople; be sure to consider nonstereotypical roles, for example, business executives who are women, or day-care workers who are men.

▶ You can set up an exchange with the businesspeople so that they also spend a day in the classroom.

♥ CLUE

The CLUE (Communicating, Listening, Understanding, Expressing) program is a way to make students' first drug possession offenses their last. It seems to be working. The sessions include diagnostic tests to determine participants' personalities as well as a variety of exercises addressing communication issues. Topics include communication styles, feelings, conflict resolution, self-esteem, rights and responsibilities, the effects of drug abuse, stress, leisure activities, and helping resources.

Obviously, you can facilitate your own program on communication and drug use. The interesting component of CLUE is that the family is brought into the process; the discussions of communication, conflict resolution, and rights and responsibilities in particular acquire a much richer meaning when students share the information with parents or guardians.

It has long been recognized that students who acknowledge boundaries of their behavior—for example, family rules, school guidelines—reduce their risks of becoming involved in problem behaviors such as drug use and violence. CLUE facilitates the establishment and communication of those boundaries.

Ingredients

Two facilitators
A place to hold nightly sessions

Instructions

1 Assign to the CLUE program middle school and high school students who are caught with drugs on school grounds for the first time.

2 Require that they and at least one of their parents, guardians, or other adult family members attend four two-hour nightly sessions during the week.

3 Allow room for eight students and up to 16 parents.

4 Facilitate the program about five times during the year.

Chef

Beth Ross, *director of student services,* Rockdale Public Schools, 954 North Main, Conyers, GA 30012, 770-860-4241

Nutrients

#2—Positive family communication, #11—Family boundaries, #12—School boundaries

Serves

Students, grades 6–12

Variations

▶ You can separate the program into one for high school students and another for middle school students.
▶ You can facilitate the program for all students as a preventive, rather than an interventive, measure.

▶ My Own Conflicts ◀

Describe what you would probably do and feel in each of the situations below:

CONFLICT	I AM LIKELY TO:	I FEEL:
When I hear that someone talked about me behind my back . . .		
When two friends are talking and leave me out . . .		
When someone yells at me . . .		
When someone puts me down . . .		
When someone blames me for something I did not do . . .		
When someone compares me to someone else . . .		
When a teacher/boss gives an assignment I cannot do . . .		

Compare your answers with those of your parent or child. Explain to her or him why you would act and feel that way. Come to an agreement about what you both think would be best to do.

FOSTER GRANDPARENTS

Westmoreland, Kansas, is a small town of about 600 people; Westmoreland Elementary School has about 175 K–6 students. Sometimes in small communities you have to stretch resources. That's what grant coordinator Gayle Doll did when she secured a grant from the Kansas Health Foundation: Personal Actions To Health (PATH) is primarily intended to promote children's activities. However, there was also another different, but potentially complementary, need in the community: There was no agency to provide meals for seniors who needed them. So Doll, who was working with older adults in an exercise class, slanted the program toward helping build students' assets through their relationships with seniors. She didn't tell the seniors that they were being offered a free meal; rather, she emphasized that they'd be helping build students' assets—which, of course, was entirely true.

At the first session, one of the students said, "Oh, they brought the people from the old folks' home." A senior overheard the comment and hesitated to return, but Doll told him that that's what they were coming for—to change attitudes.

Ingredients

> *Lunch for 30 adults*
> *Access to seniors*
> *Antiques*

Instructions

1 Canvass the community to select seniors who need meals.

2 Invite those seniors to lunch at the school every Friday, but make one particular Friday a month their "day"; consider arranging transportation, if possible.

3 Choose students from a different grade level each time, and pair them up with the seniors.

4 When the seniors come to the school, at about 11:30, introduce them to their partners, and serve everyone lunch family style.

5 Bring in an antique (e.g., a kerosene lamp), let students guess what it is, and then give opportunities for seniors to tell stories relating to it.

6 Follow lunch with recess and then an activity, for example, making ice cream, going to the gym, or attending music class.

Chef

Gayle Doll, *grant coordinator,* Pottawatomie County Extension, P.O. Box 127, Westmoreland, KS 66549, 785-457-3319

Nutrients

#3—Other adult relationships, #33—Interpersonal competence, #22—School engagement

Serves

30 students, grades K–6

Variations

▶ You can give students opportunities to invite their grandparents or elderly neighbors.
▶ You can match seniors with specific classes and lessons based on their experience, for example, musicians for music lessons, or engineers for math lessons.

THE HERO PROGRAM

Now in its fourth year, the HERO (Helping Early Readers One on One) program was created by Gary Boggs, a football coach at Fort Vancouver High School (about 1,500 students) in Vancouver, Washington. Boggs thought that his students "needed to be more than jocks" and so started what eventually became a program involving more than 100 students.

As is the case with successful mentoring or tutoring programs, both the tutors and the tutees flourish. Jan Redding, a partnership specialist in the school district, says that when the athletes enter the lunchroom, they're often asked for autographs; "they think they've died and gone to heaven." One specific success story centered on an athlete with attention deficit disorder. He was paired with half an elementary physical education class. He organized group games and channeled his disability into facilitating activities that helped everyone excel. A testimonial comes from Dusty Cruzen, who's 16 and who taught a seven-year-old to play educational video games. "I love this program," he says. "When you come, the look on their face is worth it all." There's no doubt that these athletes are role models.

Ingredients

A room with books, games, toys, and other things conducive to elementary school students learning to read, write, and accomplish other language arts tasks
Transportation from the high school to the elementary school

Instructions

1 Choose high school athletes to be tutors for students at a local elementary school. The athletes should have the following characteristics:
▶ They're committed to school;
▶ They maintain at least a C average; and
▶ They have permission from their coach, their parents, and their teachers to devote several hours a week to tutoring.

2 Choose elementary school students who need help reading. Rotate grade levels year to year.

3 Once a week, just before lunch, bring the athletes to the elementary school. Have them wear their jerseys, letter jackets, lapel pins, or something similar that identifies them.

4 When the athletes get to the elementary school, assemble everyone in the cafeteria and pair the athletes with the students for lunch and conversation.

5 After lunch, move everyone to the "reading room" or some other multipurpose room for an hour of one-to-one activities that strengthen reading, writing, and language arts in general. Supervise the activities in order to maintain discipline.

6 After an hour, have athletes walk the students back to class.

Chef

Jan Redding, *partnership specialist,* Community Partnerships Office, Vancouver School District, P.O. Box 8937, Vancouver, WA 98668, 360-313-4722

Nutrients

#18—Youth programs, #25—Reading for pleasure, #21—Achievement motivation

Serves

60 high school athletes and 60 elementary school students

Variations

▶ Cross-age tutoring is a strategy that you can use in many different forms; for example, you may want to pair middle school students with elementary school students.

▶ You can also give high school service clubs the opportunity to tutor elementary school students, or open the activity to intramural athletes as well.

 EXTRA HELPINGS for *The HERO Program: Excerpts from the Fort Vancouver High School HERO packet.*

▶ The Responsibilities of a HERO ◀

Being a HERO is a privilege. It is also a position requiring dependability and trust. In addition to following basic rules of the school and the classroom you will be working in, there are two very important things to do as a HERO:

1. You are responsible first to your own teachers. . . .Therefore, it is very important that you keep your classroom work caught up and that you are doing quality work. If your class work is suffering, you may need to take a break from the HERO program until you are caught up.

2. It is most important that you respect the student you are helping as well as other students. The work your student does with you, how s/he is doing, and anything personal your students may tell you must be kept confidential. However, any concerns you have that s/he might have shared with your during your time together, please be certain to tell the teacher. It is equally as important to share any successes and daily feedback with the teacher so that s/he might better define the program for the student you are working with.

▶ HERO Reflections ◀

Here are the questions from the HERO Reflections survey; participants need to complete the survey three times—at the beginning, middle, and end of their tutoring experience. The "Reflections" are intended to give feedback both to the program and to the participants

1. In what ways did you help the student(s) with whom you worked?

2. Did you encounter problems with your student's behavior? What actions did you take?

3. What would help you improve your skills as a tutor? What were the activities, books, or ideas that you felt worked best?

4. Describe in detail what it felt like to be a HERO to your lunch buddy.

KIDS AS SHOPPERS

After students at Eastmont Junior High School, in East Wenatchee, Washington, saw their results from the *Search Institute Profiles of Student Life: Attitudes and Behaviors* self-report survey, they determined that the community didn't care about them. Upon further discussion, they said that businesses downtown and at the local mall suspected them of planning to steal things, perhaps because they wore earrings, carried backpacks, came in groups, and otherwise manifested behaviors considered negative by the merchants. They decided to do something positive about the situation, and this is what they did.

Ingredients

Materials for constructing and implementing surveys
Liaisons with community leaders

Instructions

1 Provide opportunities for students to discuss the situation with downtown leaders and exchange views.

2 Construct a survey in which students are asked to state their shopping preferences—where they like to shop, what they like to purchase, when they like to shop, and so on.

3 Administer the survey to students.

4 Compile and analyze the results.

5 Present the results to the downtown association; plan how to translate the results into policies that provide a friendlier environment in which young people can shop.

Chef

Fran Hogan, *coordinator,* Kids First, P.O. Box 5581, Wenatchee, WA 98807, 509-665-2434, x221, kids1st@nwi.net

Nutrients

#7—Community values youth, #37—Personal power, #32—Planning and decision making

Serves

Over 600 students, grades 7–9

Variations

▶ You can address many issues with the same basic formula: Discuss the issue among all concerned parties; gather data via surveys; share the results; and plan to resolve any conflicts based on new understandings.

▶ You can survey the adults as well, so that everyone has an opportunity to see everyone else's viewpoint.

 **See EXTRA HELPINGS**

▶ Teen Shopping Survey ◀

1. What is your age? _____

2. Are you employed? _____ yes _____ no

3. What are your hobbies? _____
   _____
   _____
   _____
   _____

4. What is your main method of transportation? _____ car _____ bicycle _____ in-line skates
   _____ skateboard _____ LINK _____ other: _____

5. Where do you like to meet with friends? _____

6. Where do you shop most frequently? _____ Wenatchee Valley Mall
   _____ Valley North Mall _____ downtown _____ other: _____

7. How much do you spend on an average shopping trip? $_____

8. What is your favorite store? _____
   Why? _____
   _____
   _____

9. Do you have a favorite downtown store? If so, which one? What do you like about it? _____
   _____
   _____

10. If you do not shop downtown, please tell us why. _____
    _____
    _____

11. What types of restaurants, stores, activities, or recreational opportunities would you like to see downtown?
    _____
    _____

12. Have you or any of your family ever attended any of the following events?
    _____ Thursday market _____ outdoor concerts _____ Farmer's Market
    _____ community Christmas tree lighting _____ St. Patrick's Day parade
    _____ Trick or Treat on the Avenue _____ downtown Easter basket hunt

13. How often do you visit downtown? _____ never _____ 1-3 times/year
    _____ 4-6 times/year _____ 7-10 times/year _____ more than 10 times/year

14. Please describe your *dream downtown!* _____
    _____
    _____

We value your opinions and thank you for taking the time to give us your feedback! Please return this to the drop-off box or the Kids First Survey Team by April 19th.

KIDS IN THE HALL

This is one of those great programs that combine many positive features: providing a friendly school environment; establishing and maintaining good student-adult relationships; and, of course, spreading appreciation of reading. The activity symbolizes what education at its best is all about: the enjoyment of gaining knowledge and skills, and the sharing of that enjoyment with others.

School social worker Jim Williams reports a general improvement in reading scores, but he says that what's most impressive is that students are now reading more on their own, they're more excited about reading, and it doesn't seem to be a chore. He adds that if you walk down the halls and students know you, they'll stop you and show you what they're reading.

Ingredients

A brochure describing the program

One cart of 50–60 age-appropriate books for each classroom

One hall monitor for several classrooms

Urns of coffee and hot water for tea, as well as cups, teabags, stirrers, milk, sweeteners, napkins, paper towels, and so on

Couches and comfortable chairs

Instructions

1 Have teachers visit with the parents of all 1st-grade students on one evening at the beginning of the year and give out a brochure about the reading program. Continue to publicize the program in other ways.

2 Make available a cart of age-appropriate books for each classroom.

3 Set up a time before school—say, between 8:00 and 8:30—when students come into the hallway or sit in front of their classrooms, and read books or magazines.

4 Encourage parents and other adults who bring their children to school to stay and read as well.

5 Allow students to read what they bring from home, get from the library, or take from the classroom cart.

6 One or two days a week, provide for parents urns of coffee and hot water for tea at the entrance to the school, in addition to couches and chairs.

7 Assign adult monitors to help students read, prevent squabbles, and maintain order.

Chef

Jim Williams, *school social worker,* Westwood Elementary School, 1600 North Eisenhower Drive, Junction City, KS 66441, 785-238-2840

Nutrients

#25—Reading for pleasure, #6—Parent involvement in schooling, #5—Caring school climate

Serves

330 students, grades K–5

Variations

▶ You can expand the program to after school as well.

▶ You can provide opportunities for cross-age teaching.

♥ KINDNESS CHAINS

Despite her efforts, preschool teacher Yvette Zaepfel saw that her charges were being mean to each other. When she tried explaining to them that they were being mean, they responded, in so many words, "Well, that was the point." Then Zaepfel took a different tack: Instead of focusing on reducing the negative behavior, she initiated a strategy to increase positive behavior and, indeed, to make it a habit. The goals of Kindness Chains are to increase the frequency of kind acts and also help the children remember them. The chains usually take at least a month to complete; once, Zaepfel had a chain with 182 loops.

Zaepfel reports, however, that children can take advantage of this system, and monitoring is necessary: One time she saw a girl knock over some crayons on purpose, just so she could put them away and get a strip. And another time, she saw two children help each other with their nap mats (when they were perfectly capable of arranging their own) in order to get two strips.

But most of the time, the kindness chains activity is a prototypical example of the asset framework in action: Young people's strengths are identified and encouraged, when it would be easy to focus on discipline and punishment.

Ingredients

Paper, scissors, and tape

Instructions

1 Cut colored paper into strips of about 8 ½ inches x 1 inch.

2 After someone does something kind—the act can be self- or other-reported—write the act on the strip of paper and then tape one end to the other in a loop. Tape the first loop to the wall. Some examples of "kind acts":

▶ "Cole helped a shorter child get her cubby down."

▶ "Stuart fell on the ground, and, even though she

didn't cause it, Samantha picked him up and gave him a hug."

▶ "Carolyn cleaned up a block area that she wasn't even playing in."

▶ "Without being asked, Molly offered half her muffin to Adam when we ran out."

3 Try to see that everyone gets strips; use lower criteria for children who have a harder time being kind and watch them carefully to make sure that they have an opportunity to get strips, too.

4 Continue in this fashion until the loops accumulate into a "kindness chain."

5 Designate the other end of the room or some other place as a goal, and have a party when the chain reaches the goal.

6 At the party, return all the strips to the children who committed the kind acts.

Chef

Yvette Zaepfel, *lead preschool teacher,* Kidspace, 3837 13th Avenue West, Seattle, WA 98119, 206-282-3622

Nutrients

#26—Caring, #12—School boundaries, #15—Positive peer influence

Serves

14 students, preschool

Variations

▶ Although this was born as a preschool activity, you can use it at any grade level. The two variables are what determines acts of kindness and how those acts should be represented. In elementary school, an act of kindness might be lending a classmate a certain color crayon or volunteering to help the teacher collect homework. In middle school/junior high school, it might be sticking up for someone being bullied on the playground or inviting a new student to participate in an activity. And in high school, it might be donating used CDs to the library or offering to tutor a classmate.

▶ Some teachers who have adopted this strategy use jars of marbles instead of strips, but you can use whatever seems appropriate to your resources and grade level: blocks across the floor, stars on a chart, lines on a graph, or even miles along a map route (the party could take on the flavor of the destination city).

🍎 LEARN TO EARN

This is a good example of a faith community extending what students learn in school by providing opportunities for academic learning, sustenance, relationships, and job skills. The First Presbyterian Church of Orlando—with about 5,000 members—works with Howard Middle School to provide one-on-one mentoring for 30 students on the Free Lunch program. The Learn to Earn program is an off-shoot of this; students get experience working at a regular "job" for tangible goods.

Ingredients

> *Refurbished bicycles, helmets, chains, and locks*
> *Meals*
> *Certificates*
> *Mentors*
> *A community center, with rooms containing books, games, desks, chairs, and other equipment*

Instructions

1 Identify students (e.g., those from disadvantaged families) to participate in the program.

2 Pick up the students after school and bring them to the church.

3 Greet the students, have them wash their hands, and give them a meal, for example, hamburger, carrots, grapes, a drink, and dessert.

4 Spend the next 45 minutes either doing homework, writing thank-you notes to people, or participating in some other activity relating to schoolwork or academic skills.

5 After this, provide opportunities for students to participate in elective activities (e.g., gym, computer lab, or job training).

6 Provide opportunities for some of these students to "learn to earn":
- ▶ They show up every Wednesday evening for two hours, five weeks in a row.
- ▶ They work in a kitchen or in the financial office or some other on-site office.
- ▶ They get paid the equivalent of minimum wage in refurbished bicycles, helmets, chains, and locks provided by the local police station.
- ▶ They earn a certificate for satisfactorily completing the program.

Chef

Jean Huddleston, *director of the after-school outreach ministry,* First Presbyterian Church of Orlando, 106 East Church Street, Orlando, FL 32801, 407-206-2406

Nutrients

#18—Youth programs, #13—Neighborhood boundaries, #23—Homework

Serves

30 students, grades 6–8

Variations

- ▶ The faith community can act as a liaison between school and businesses, setting up some students as part-time workers.
- ▶ The faith community can offer "study halls" on weekends to students whose family situations aren't conducive to studying.

LEARNING TO VOLUNTEER

Sometimes we take volunteering for granted, but Learning to Volunteer actually paves the way for volunteering—from both ends. As a result of a community forum on volunteerism, 30 to 40 students from grades 5–12 got together and lamented the negative image of young people in the community and in the media. They wanted to clear up their image and also do things for the community, declaring that it was "cool to care." Thus, the activity was created, originally involving 18 nonprofit agencies, an education class from Colorado State University, and 8–10 7th-grade students at Lincoln Junior High School.

Ingredients

Access to local nonprofit agencies
Access to a university education class
Knowledge about working with young volunteers

Instructions

1 Give a half-day workshop to representatives from local nonprofit agencies on how to use young people as volunteers; include such topics as legal liabilities.

2 Contact an education class from a local university, and offer teacher candidates hands-on learning by mentoring students; visit the class to provide information about mentoring.

3 Have the mentors visit students at school and plan projects:

▶ First, a project involving everyone (e.g., working at an Alzheimer's Association Memory Walk);

▶ Then, a project involving small groups (e.g., working at a homeless shelter or food bank); and

▶ Finally, a project in which students volunteer on their own.

Chef

Patti Schmitt, *development coordinator,* FirstCall, 424 Pine Street, #103, Fort Collins, CO 80524, 970-407-7066

Nutrients

#27—Equality and social justice, #26—Caring, #8—Youth as resources

Serves

200 students, grade 7

Variations

▶ You can invite representatives from local nonprofit agencies to make presentations to your students about their respective organizations.

▶ You can offer incentives for students to involve other students outside the class in their projects.

 **See EXTRA HELPINGS**

EXTRA HELPINGS for *Learning to Volunteer: Summary of agenda for half-day training on youth involvement.*

▶ *Agenda* ◀

1. "What Today's Youth Are Like"—youth discussion about why they volunteer, what they like to get involved in, and what is important to them
2. "The Importance of Youth Volunteers"—presentation on how youth can contribute
3. "Liability Issues Working with Youth Volunteers"— history of addressing liability issues, ways organizations can address the issues, and question-and-answer session facilitated by a volunteer attorney
4. "Developing Volunteer and Service-Learning Projects for Youth"—large- and small-group discussions about how agencies can develop projects for youth
5. "What Is the Difference between Service-Learning and Volunteering, and How Do I Do It?"—discussion of how to organize a service-learning project
6. "Generating Sustainable Youth Volunteers"—presentation by youth and adults on how to keep youth volunteers returning
7. "Closing and Action Plan"—reflection and sharing about how more youth can be brought into organizations

♥ LUNCH BUDDIES

Mentoring programs aren't really unusual, but this one is different because of who's involved—office staff from a state department, specifically, the South Carolina Department of Health and Environmental Control. Robert Carlton, director of youth development for the department, wanted to contribute to the local school district. He coordinated a lunch-mentoring program with 2nd-grade students (60–70 percent of them on free or reduced-cost lunch) at H. B. Rhame Elementary School in Columbia; to his surprise, 70 people volunteered from his department.

Carlton reports that both students and adults look forward to the days—the first and third Thursday each month—when the bus carrying the mentors arrives at the school. "The adults gain as much as the children," he says, especially because many of them have desk jobs and, except for those with their own children, have had no other contact with kids, certainly not in schools.

There are many types of "lunch mentoring" programs around the country. One, "The Lunch Bunch," is directed by Judy Alig, in rural Ulysses, Kansas (316-356-1830); it serves about 60 students in grades 5–8. An interesting feature of "The Lunch Bunch" is that occasionally they hold lunch meetings at the various participating businesses.

Ingredients

Transportation between workplace and school
Training of mentors
Coordination to pair mentors with students

Instructions

1 Ask around to find a business or government organization interested in doing this at your school.

2 Solicit volunteers from the business to be lunchtime mentors with students; compile both a main and a substitute list.

3 Give the volunteers an hour-long orientation about their roles and responsibilities.

4 Arrange for a school bus to pick up the mentors and take them to the school.

5 Have the mentors eat lunch in the cafeteria with their assigned student (e.g., all the 2nd-grade students) and then move to the classroom, either to do reading and writing or something related to a character-education attribute, for example, honesty or responsibility.

6 Arrange for a "shadowing" day, in which students are taken to the mentors' workplace and ask them about what they do and what education they have.

7 Try to keep the same mentor-student pairings from 2nd grade through 5th grade.

Chef

Robert Carlton, *director of youth development,* South Carolina Department of Health and Environmental Control, 1751 Calhoun Street, Columbia, SC 29201, 803-898-0302

Nutrients

#3—Other adult relationships, #14—Adult role models, #21—Achievement motivation

Serves

70 students, grades 2–5 (progressively)

Variations

▶ Instead of lunch, you can hold the mentoring session at other times of the day.
▶ You can target specific academic subjects for mentoring, depending on the source of the mentors.

♥ MATH BUDDIES

"We want to promote a community of learners," says Joanne Tuxbury, and that's just what she and her colleague, Muriel Bergeron, have done in a small school in New Hampshire with their Math Buddies program. The core of the program is the community of Tuxbury's 4th-grade class and Bergeron's 2nd-grade class. By combining the classes and encouraging the students to teach and work with each other, the two teachers have produced something quite extraordinary. Their students had been reading to each other for some time, but, says Tuxbury, "we wanted more." One of the things they wanted was to enhance their math curriculum.

They did. Math Buddies has seen students progress much further than one would typically expect: They use Polydron kits (see www.polydron.com on the Web) to produce complex three-dimensional shapes. They create a "geo-dictionary" that defines geometric terms. They develop and host their own stations at a Family Math Night. By treating each student as a resource, by bringing classmates and family members into the learning equation, and by motivating their students to achieve more than the students ever thought they could, Tuxbury and Bergeron have indeed created a learning community—as well as a teaching community.

Ingredients

Books with mathematical themes in the narrative
Materials for geometry classes
Publishing materials (e.g., paper, computer, printer, bookbinding supplies)
Coordination between two classrooms
Adult and student volunteers to plan and facilitate a family event

Instructions

1 Once a week, for about 50 minutes, combine a 4th-grade class with a 2nd-grade class, and encourage the 4th-grade students to read to the 2nd-grade students (link students one to one as much as possible, avoiding sibling matches); focus on literature that has some mathematical theme as part of the story; gradually introduce strategy games to the curriculum.

2 Teach geometry to the classes separately, at the appropriate grade levels.

3 After about a month, introduce manipulatives to the combined class so that they can make different two- and three-dimensional shapes and begin composing a "geo-dictionary," a dictionary of geometric terms.

4 Have them write and type the entries in the dictionary, and publish the final product.

5 Have students host a Family Math Night, in which they devise activities and teach them at various stations to parents and others.

Chefs

Joanne Tuxbury, *teacher,* Sunapee Central Elementary School, 22 School Street, Sunapee, NH 03782, 603-763-5675, jtuxbury@sunapee.k12.nh.us; **Muriel Bergeron,** *teacher,* Sunapee Central Elementary School, 22 School Street, Sunapee, NH 03782, 603-763-5675, mbergeron@sunapee.k12.nh.us

Nutrients

#21—Achievement motivation, #6—Parent involvement in schooling, #33—Interpersonal competence

Serves

19 students, grade 4, and 17 students, grade 2

Variations

▶ You can combine other classrooms for similar activities, in math or other disciplines.

▶ You can supplement the classes by bringing in mathematicians, engineers, chefs, designers, or other professionals who use mathematics as part of their jobs.

MINISTRY TO NEIGHBORHOOD CHILDREN

This program started when St. Paul Lutheran Church, an 1840 structure just behind the French Quarter in New Orleans, was visited by a group of about eight children from a rather dysfunctional family; they came without their parents and misbehaved in front of the congregation. The pastor and others took them aside and explained to them kindly about the church and church behavior. Soon, more children started to come on their own. The church set up a tutoring program to help the children with their homework. More people volunteered to help, more children came, and the program grew. What started as an informal relationship with a few children has metamorphosed into a systematic program in which many children are taught and cared for.

Ingredients

Volunteers to be tutors and mentors

A place to meet

Activities

Instructions

1 Contact community congregations, and arrange to set up a tutoring program (e.g., on Monday evenings from 5:30 to 6:30) for neighborhood youth with volunteers from the faith community. Tie in the tutoring with the young people's specific academic requirements.

2 Train the volunteers, and hold monthly meetings in which the adults can discuss the status of the program, ways to improve, and so on.

3 Augment the tutoring with "social mentoring," in which the adults can take the youth, for example, to the zoo, or to a fast-food restaurant, or to an art museum.

4 Facilitate auxiliary activities, such as a sit-down dinner at which the youth can learn or practice table manners.

5 Adapt the tutoring to the young people's needs, for example, by teaching basic skills via phonics, teaching the recognition of functional signs with flash cards (e.g., "stop," "yield," "no parking"), or teaching sewing.

6 Establish the appropriate liaisons with both schools and families to coordinate the tutoring and the "social mentoring."

Chefs

Leo and Rose Merle Symmank, 6844 Louis XIV Street, New Orleans, LA 70124, 504-488-9491; **Eileen Stensrud,** 25 Chamale Cove, Slidell, LA 70460, 504-645-0311

Nutrients

#19—Religious community, #3—Other adult relationships, #21—Achievement motivation

Serves

24 students, grades K–12

Variations

▶ Although in some cases the reason for the children's approaching the faith community is a lack of parental supervision, in other cases you can include the parents in the activities—and you should probably try to do so in all cases.

▶ You can also set up peer-helping sessions so that the children form a support network of their own.

THE PROUD PANTHER

Hope Bosworth wanted to do something for the elementary school students in Springdale, Arkansas, that would not only "make a difference" but also be an ongoing activity, continually involving the students. So Bosworth helped start a newspaper.

The newspaper, *The Proud Panther*, raises funds for charities, but, just as important, it gives students opportunities to contribute meaningfully—in the production of the newspaper and in the serving of the charities. The first edition of *The Proud Panther*—with its 12 reporters from grades 3–5 writing stories on topics including a national election, the Olympics, and the benefiting charity—sold 250 copies (in a school of about 330 students). The benefiting charity was Lifestyles, a home that helps the mentally and physically handicapped to live independently. Students were able to purchase a park bench as well as flowers, which they helped plant on a Saturday in October. Proceeds from the most recent edition of the paper have gone to help the Cancer Support House, a home that provides assistance, education, nutritional information, overnight accommodations, wigs, and other services to people in the Springdale community with cancer.

As coordinator and senior editor of *The Proud Panther*, Bosworth conducts the research into charities, meets with reporters to review their work, and sets up the newspaper for publication. She also accompanies student editors and reporters, as well as Principal Maribel Childress, to the benefiting charity, where the students present their gift and learn firsthand how they're helping people in their community.

Ingredients

Several staff to be editors, and several students to be reporters

Materials and equipment to print a four-page newspaper

Access to charities

Instructions

1 Have teachers choose one student from each class to be a reporter—not necessarily the smartest or the most popular, but perhaps students who need support or recognition.

2 Assemble school adults to be editors.

3 Ask a community representative (e.g., someone from United Way) to tell the reporters about two charities with specific needs, and have the reporters vote on which of the two will benefit from the proceeds of the newspaper.

4 Brainstorm with students ideas for stories, and give them a schedule to meet with the editors; be sure that every student has one adult editor to meet with. Ask the students to give up their recesses to meet.

5 Over the course of about six weeks, have students submit a draft and then a final copy of their stories.

6 Lay out and print the newspaper, publicize it (e.g., with a note to parents), and sell it to students, for example, for 50 cents a copy.

7 With the proceeds, purchase something specific that meets the needs of the chosen charity, and then have the reporters spend part of a day at the charity to see the effect of their work.

8 Choose new reporters for the next issue of the paper.

Chef

Hope Bosworth, c/o Parson Hills Elementary School, 2326 Cardinal, Springdale, AR 72764, 501-750-8877, parsonnews@hotmail.com

Nutrients

#26—Caring, #17—Creative activities, #22—School engagement

Serves

330 students, grades 3–5

Variations

▶ You can adapt this idea to almost any grade level; the point is to involve students who may not normally participate in activities like this.

▶ Increase the publicity and expand the readership to the community at large. You can publicize the event at the charity, at least in the next issue of the paper.

THE RACE, CULTURE, AND ETHNICITY WORKSHOP

"It's always interesting to see students come in at 9:00 on the Saturday morning when we have the workshop and they are very nervous and excited, but they don't know what to expect. They huddle in different spaces with others from their school and are afraid to venture out of their space to meet new people. However, when the workshop ends around 3:30, everybody is talking, exchanging telephone numbers, sitting with people from other schools, and starting new friendships. The whole idea is to bring people together and celebrate our humanity."

So says Professor Pharnal Longus of Salem State College, Salem, Massachusetts, who has been facilitating this workshop in one form or another since 1972. He's expanded his college course into a one-day workshop—once in October and again in February—for high school students, and the results have been positive all along. The workshop aims at more than reducing conflicts peacefully; it strives to foster a "cultural understanding."

The idea behind presenting this activity is not necessarily to replicate Professor Longus's workshop; rather, it's to make available a workshop with the same objectives for the same audience—to make use of college resources to improve high school environments.

Ingredients

A workshop design, materials, space, and a facilitator
Money for lunch, snacks, and materials
Publicity

Instructions

1 Contact a local college or university to see whether they'd be interested in doing this project.

2 Ask them to design a workshop for high school students with the following learning objectives:
▶ To define the concepts of race, culture, and ethnicity
▶ To get to know people from other schools
▶ To put into practice what they've learned when they return to their schools

3 Make the workshop interactive, practical, and relevant to important social issues that high school students currently face.

4 Solicit participation from local high schools:
▶ Five to 20 students
▶ One educator for every five students
▶ Students to be representative of racial, ethnic, and cultural groups in their school

5 Charge each student just enough to cover lunch, snacks, and materials.

6 Require the educators to attend one seminar before the workshop to clarify concepts, goals, and objectives.

Chef

Pharnal Longus, *professor,* School of Social Work, Salem State College, Salem, MA 01970, 978-542-6816, www.mclanedesigns.com/workshop, pharnal.longus@salem.mass.edu or longus@massed.net

Nutrients

#34—Cultural competence, #33—Interpersonal competence, #36—Peaceful conflict resolution

Serves

Up to 80 students, grades 9–12

Variations

▶ You can ask high school students to cofacilitate the workshop; you can facilitate this type of workshop for all age-groups.
▶ If you don't have access to a college or university, you can change the tenor of the workshop to "controlled discussions," in which people can share their experiences and insights into cultural issues.

 **READ**

READ stands for Reading Encourages All Dreams, and it's the fruition of a dream by 15-year-old Kyle Alderson of Muldrow, Oklahoma. Alderson enjoys reading, and he wanted to do something that would combine that enjoyment with helping others. So, with help from his mother, Miki, he started a mentoring program for children who have been having difficulty reading. He worked with the local library, his own high school, and the local elementary school to get the program going, and he sought and was awarded a $1,000 "Make a Difference Day" (a national event—see www.makeadifferenceday.com on the Web) grant from the Wal-Mart company to purchase instruction manuals and books.

Young Alderson says that the program—which so far involves 20 high school mentors and 35 elementary school students—has seen both an improvement in the young students' reading and a growing relationship between them and their mentors. It's another testament to the resourcefulness of young people and their ability to initiate and manage programs that benefit others.

Ingredients

Liaison with local library
Access to high school to recruit mentors
Access to elementary school to solicit participants

Instructions

1 Contact the local library to get its cooperation in providing a space and time for mentors.

2 Get permission from the local high school to recruit mentors, for example, via flyers and discussions with students:

▶ Students who are doing well academically
▶ Students who are willing to devote time to be a mentor
▶ Students who receive a recommendation from their teacher

3 Solicit participants from the local elementary school:

▶ Students who need extra help reading
▶ Students whose parents or other family members can take them to and from the library

4 Coordinate with elementary school teachers or librarians to secure reading lists for the appropriate grade levels.

5 Provide an orientation—perhaps an hour—for the mentors.

6 Have mentors meet their students at the library once or twice a week, from 30 to 60 minutes, throughout the year. Suggest that they not only take turns reading but also play games (e.g., checkers) and hold conversations to prevent the students from becoming bored.

Chef

Kyle Alderson, 503 Juniper Lane, Muldrow, OK 74948, 918-427-7227

Nutrients

#25—Reading for pleasure, #15—Positive peer influence, #30—Responsibility

Serves

20 students, grades 9–12; 35 students, grades K–4

Variations

▶ You can have mentors meet students at the students' homes.
▶ You can hold an event at the end of, say, six months, in which the students take turns reading aloud to show their progress.

SAVE ONE STUDENT

The critical component of programs like Save One Student—now in its fourth year—is the recognition that all school adults are potentially involved in establishing supportive relationships with students. Save One Student also recognizes an important factor in mentoring: that students have different needs. Some of the needs are financial, others supportive, still others intellectual. This program allows for a variety of types of support for students; it could be helping out with purchasing school supplies, touching base during report card time, or meeting with them to discuss problems. The key is that the relationship is genuine and supportive.

Ingredients

Volunteers to be mentors
Coordination between staff and students

Instructions

1 At the end of the year, have teachers identify students who are having academic or behavioral problems or who need more support than perhaps they're getting at home. Add names at the beginning of the following year.

2 Ask all staff members—including cafeteria workers, bus drivers, and clerical staff—to volunteer to be "buddies" to the students, one to one. Give staff the opportunity to identify students, too.

3 Give an orientation to the volunteers about their roles and responsibilities.

4 Contact the students and their parents to determine what they need in terms of support, supplies, and so on.

5 Establish criteria for when staff members interact with students and what kinds of support they give them.

Chefs

Cindy Talbert, *principal,* and **Margaret Lopatka,** *counselor,* Ogden Elementary School, 3637 Middle Sound Loop Road, Wilmington, NC 28411, 910-686-9506

Nutrients

#3—Other adult relationships, #5—Caring school climate, #21—Achievement motivation

Serves

35 students, grades K–5

Variations

▶ You can give students the opportunity to choose from a field of volunteer school adults.
▶ You can set aside times for meetings between the student and the school adult.

THE SCHOOL ON WHEELS

McConnelsville, Ohio, is a very poor and rugged community in Appalachia, and many of the incoming kindergartners are, academically, one to two years behind where they ought to be. Families often don't have transportation, and, even though there are about 200 four-year-olds in the county, the only preschool is for disabled children. Howard Troutner, director of school improvement at Morgan Local Schools, secured a federal Reading Excellence Act grant and with some of the money purchased a used motor home—a 23-foot 1989 Allegro with 60,000 miles on it. He hired an early childhood specialist and teacher aide, who then helped design the inside of the van, now called the School on Wheels.

The School on Wheels currently serves about 40–45 four-year-olds, traveling about 80–100 miles a day and meeting with perhaps 40 families each week. To avoid intruding on the parents' privacy, Troutner outfitted the van so that families do all the activities inside the van, not inside their homes.

Ingredients

A van, stocked with preschool materials
An early childhood specialist
A teacher's aide

Instructions

1 Make 30-minute weekly visits to the families with preschool-aged children; invite the parent(s), the child, and any younger siblings into the van.

A mobile classroom takes learning to the children.

2 In a carpeted play area in the back of the van, have the aide spend time with the siblings.

3 In the main part of the van, have the teacher work alongside the parent(s) with the child on preschool activities, for example:

▶ Singing
▶ Hand-eye coordination
▶ Letter and number recognition

4 Provide a computer in the van to keep track of children's progress.

5 Lend and give out materials, for example, games, books, videotapes, audiotapes, and parenting products.

Chef

Howard Troutner, *director of school improvement,* Morgan Local Schools, 78 East Main Street, McConnelsville, OH 43756, 740-962-2377

Nutrients

#6—Parent involvement in schooling, #5—Caring school climate, #16—High expectations

Serves

45 children, preschool

Variations

▶ Although the School on Wheels is perfectly adapted to this community, you can make modifications based on the community you're serving; for example, your van could travel a certain route every day and offer similar services to preschool-aged children and their families.
▶ You can even take the targeted age-group lower, for example, by focusing on toddlers (or even younger—"waddlers").

SCHOOL-GROWN VEGETABLES

This is an example of a garden project that can be done on a small scale but that can have great benefits. There are about 715 students, grades K–5, at Mauka Lani Elementary School, and, according to PTA Projects Officer Sharon Nakamura, most of them had never grown a plant until they worked in this garden project, which was started by a group of teachers about six years ago on a 28' x 36' plot on the school grounds. In this section of Hawaii—the southern end of the Waianae mountain range on the island of Oahu—very few families have backyard gardens, and, aside from pineapples and bananas, home-grown fruit and vegetables are rare. Nakamura, who is from Chicago, is restructuring the current garden into two 12' x 36' plots reinforced by railroad ties (first, though, she had to explain to students what railroad ties were).

The garden has many uses. Many of the classrooms rotate responsibilities for watering, tending, and harvesting the vegetables (mostly mustard cabbage, soy beans, and green beans); the teachers work the responsibilities into their respective curricula; and, come harvest time, students take home "school-grown" vegetables to their families. Each class also cooks a meal using its own crop.

Ingredients

Gardening materials, including seeds and equipment
Coordination with classroom curricula

Instructions

1 Secure plots for growing vegetables.

2 Solicit volunteers from teachers as well as high school students (e.g., from Future Farmers of America), the latter of whom can act as mentors to the elementary school students.

3 Coordinate with teachers and their classes to determine what to plant and how to rotate responsibility for the care of the garden.

Railroad ties mark out the plots for the students' garden.

4 Incorporate the responsibilities into class work, for example, mathematics, science, and agriculture.

5 Harvest the vegetables and allow students and school staff to bring them home.

Chef

Sharon Nakamura, *projects officer,* Mauka Lani PTA, Mauka Lani Elementary School, 92-1300 Panana Street, Kapolei, HI 96707, 808-672-1100

Nutrients

#22—School engagement, #8—Youth as resources, #32—Planning and decision making

Serves

As many classrooms as want to participate, given the size of the plot and the yield

Variations

▶ You can have classrooms take responsibility for specific areas of the garden.
▶ You can hold a dinner for school families that features vegetables from the garden, or provide adjuncts to school lunches.

SENIORS ON THE INTERNET

One of the students in a service-learning class at Project Ready, a 66-student alternative school for at-risk kids in Bettendorf, Iowa, had worked in a home for the elderly. He came up with the idea to teach seniors how to access the Internet. Seven students helped acquire a computer lab at the area education agency with 22 computers. They then acquired the services of a volunteer from a local computer store to facilitate a workshop.

The workshop was a terrific success. The students dressed in their best clothes for the seniors, and the student in charge of the meal—who later became a chef (a food chef, not an activity chef)—paid particular attention to finding out what the seniors liked to eat and preparing something nutritious. The seniors looked up gardening, stocks, travel, and other subjects. "We just had fun together," said Linda Goff, adviser to the project. She said that the students were touched that the seniors were complimentary to them.

Ingredients

Computers
A computer specialist
A room for a workshop

Instructions

1 Gain the use of a computer lab.

2 Solicit the services of a volunteer from a local computer store to facilitate a 45- to 60-minute workshop on the basics of using the Internet.

3 Arrange publicity for the workshop through e-mail, employers, radio, and the newspaper; take reservations for the workshop from any interested senior citizen (self-defined).

4 Have students give a demonstration of the Internet following the workshop.

5 Give the participants about two hours in the computer lab to apply what they've learned. Provide lunch as well.

Chef

Linda Goff, Bettendorf Middle School, 2030 Middle Road, Bettendorf, IA 52722, 319-359-3686

Nutrients

#26—Caring, #8—Youth as resources, #22—School engagement

Serves

Seven students, grades 10–12

Variations

▶ You can train students to facilitate the entire workshop, and you can then expand the workshop to other segments of the population.

▶ You can identify segments of the population who aren't that mobile and send students out with laptops to facilitate the workshop; you can ask computer stores to donate computers in exchange for the publicity.

♥ SHARE A FRIEND

Of all the activities in this book, this might be the most "special," even though that word is overused. It's not because the activity pairs students with handicapped adults, though that's laudable. It's not even because the activity continues to grow and thrive, though that's exciting. This activity is special because the originator and coordinator of Share a Friend is 13 years old. His name is Michael Kent Kay.

Kay's younger brother was "almost totally disabled," and it struck him that he'd like to do something for the physically and mentally disabled people in his community. He contacted a nearby residential group home and proposed his plan. He then recruited some of the members of his 4-H club. As the idea and the project grew, Kay talked with other youth groups in his community. There are now 61 disabled adult-student pairs in Share a Friend, and the number grows.

Kay sees a twofold purpose to Share a Friend. One is to provide companionship to people who may find that it's at a premium. The other is perhaps even more important in the long run, and that's to remove the fear and nervousness that frequently surround disabled people. "We hope to make them feel like part of the community as well as make the general public realize that disabled people are just like us," says Kay. "Just because someone is different, you don't have to fear them." He's already seen the philosophy work. One girl in his 4-H club was initially afraid to meet her new friend. Soon, though, and despite the fact that the program is set up to foster one-to-one relationships, she asked for two more friends from the home.

Kay's brother, the inspiration for this program, died in February 2001; at that time, the Share a Friend program became the 4-H Share a Friend Foundation in Memory of Julian Kyle Kay.

Ingredients

> *Access to youth organizations*
> *Liaisons with residential group homes for the disabled*

Instructions

1 Work with youth organizations (e.g., 4-H and Girl Scouts) to enlist young people who want to befriend a handicapped adult.

2 Contact residential group homes for the disabled and solicit their participation.

3 Based on mutual interests, link the students with the handicapped adults.

4 Provide an orientation for the students.

5 Ask that students spend at least an hour with their new friends at least once a month at least throughout the year.

6 Coordinate special events (e.g., golfing or bowling outings) with students and their new friends.

Chef

Michael Kent Kay, Illinois 4-H Foundation, 4-H Share a Friend Foundation, 21520 Elmwood Avenue, Wilmington, IL 60481, 3kay@keynet.net

Nutrients

#33—Interpersonal competence, #26—Caring, #39—Sense of purpose

Serves

60 students, grades 3–12

Variations

▶ You can coordinate this through a school at least as easily as through youth groups.

▶ You can set up projects (e.g., video interviews, collages, or written narratives) for the students and their disabled friends.

☺ A 6TH-GRADE YARN

Iola Cook saw a sign in a knitting store indicating that the store would donate quilts to needy families. She wrote a grant request to a local company to get yarn and needles, and then she secured the services of volunteers who taught her 6th-grade students to knit. Cook says that boys and girls participated with equal enthusiasm and competence. Beyond the act of directly participating in a charitable activity, her students learned a skill, and Cook has evidence of its lasting effect—a few of her students turned up in her ongoing knitting circle.

Ingredients

Yarn

Needles

Volunteers who can knit, sew, and teach

Instructions

1 Discuss with students the meaning of charity and the goal of the project.

2 Enlist volunteers to teach students to knit, with each volunteer facilitating two one-hour sessions in different parts of the school for one or two students.

3 Have students knit about 50 9" x 9" squares.

4 Ask a volunteer to sew the squares into a quilt.

5 Donate the quilt to the American Red Cross or to a homeless shelter.

Chef

Iola Cook, *teacher*, Hope Elementary School, 34 Highfield Road, Hope, ME 04847, 207-785-4081, iola_cook@fivetowns.net

Nutrients

#26—Caring, #22—School engagement, #30—Responsibility

Serves

18 students, grade 6 (the school's entire 6th grade)

Variations

▶ You can use any craft (e.g., crocheting, macramé, needlepoint) as a catalyst for creating and donating materials to the needy; consider crafts that can be mastered by any disabled students, too.

▶ You can expand the idea to the entire school, especially in the making of patchwork quilts, in which individuals, classrooms, and even grade levels can create squares reflecting their own identities, classroom topics, or interests.

☺ STUDENTS WHO CARE

Linda Cirilli teaches an 8th-grade class in family-consumer education, and she puts her teaching into action. First, the students in her class discuss doing things for the common good—the concept of "if someone is in need, then everyone is in need." They then choose a charity and launch an effort to make a meaningful contribution.

Last year students chose the Food Pantry—a local agency that gives food to the poor—and decided to do a schoolwide food drive. The drive took 10 days, and they ended up collecting about $300 in cash and over $1,000 worth of food. They then boxed up the contributions, and a volunteer drove the boxes and the students over to the Food Pantry. There they packed bags for each family, put food on shelves and in storage containers, and learned about the agency. It was the largest donation the agency had ever received.

One well-dressed woman came in to the Food Pantry with her three children and asked for food for three. When asked about her husband and herself, she replied that she needed the food only for her children; she was given food for five, anyway. Students observing or later hearing about this interaction learned three lessons: One lesson is that people in need of food may not fit any particular stereotype; a second lesson is that people may be poor—or hungry—only for a short while; and a third lesson is that people often really don't want to take charity.

This year the class is working on several different projects, among them learning to sew and making blankets for all the newborns in Rhinelander, which has a population of about 12,000.

Ingredients

Access to community agencies
Access to school administration
Transportation

Instructions

1 Invite representatives from community agencies to make presentations in class.

2 After the presentations, ask students to choose one of the groups that they feel is the neediest and that they think they can help.

3 Have students write a proposal for their project and submit it to both the principal and the school board.

4 Give students the opportunity to set up a competition for which homeroom could collect the most money or, for example, food, for the charity; publicize the competition through announcements and posters.

5 Have students follow through with the contribution by, for example, delivering the food to the agency.

6 Ask students to write about their experiences.

Chef

Linda Cirilli, *teacher,* James Williams Junior High School, 915 Acacia Lane, Rhinelander, WI 54501, 715-365-9220

Nutrients

#26—Caring, #32—Planning and decision making, #30—Responsibility

Serves

15 students, grade 8

Variations

▶ You can expand the project to the whole school by having different grade levels choose different charities. And you don't have to make it a competition; you can set some common goals—a certain amount of money, a certain amount of food—and have everyone cooperate in achieving those goals.

▶ You can ask the agency to give you a report on the effect of the students' contributions several months after the project has been completed.

THE SUNSHINE CLUB

This activity is like a two-way mentoring program. Kris Martin links up students from the 4th through 8th grades with residents of a nearby nursing home and, essentially, watches the relationships grow. At first, she said, her students were nervous and even fearful—of old people, of sickness, of nursing homes in general. But after the first visit, everything changed. What began with six students a year ago continued into the summer, even though the program officially had ended. Now there are 20 students participating in the Sunshine Club, with more on the waiting list, unable to participate only because of the limitations of transportation.

There's a waiting list at Slater Health Care, too, as the residents have learned how wonderful visits from children can be. Martin says that the visits occur in each of the residents' rooms, and that the students have become so aware of the residents as "people," they stop by on the way to their "partner's" room to say hello to other residents who aren't part of the program.

Ingredients

> *Liaison with nursing home*
> *Transportation*

Instructions

1 Contact a local nursing home or similar home for the elderly, and meet with the activities director to identify which residents would be interested in getting visits from students; determine what they'd like to do during those visits.

2 Solicit student volunteers to visit the nursing home, and link them up with specific residents depending on what the volunteer would like to do, for example, read to the resident, play cards, talk, and so on.

3 Set up visits for about an hour after school every other week.

4 Meet monthly with students as a large group to discuss what they've been doing and learning on their visits and what they might do on future visits.

Chef

Kris Martin, *teacher,* St. Cecilia School, 755 Central Avenue, Pawtucket, RI 02861, 401-723-9463

Nutrients

#33—Interpersonal competence, #30—Responsibility, #26—Caring

Serves

At least 20 students, grades 4–8

Variations

▶ You can supplement visits with weekend events, like lunches, dances, or readings.
▶ You can supplement the individual relationships by forming small groups, say, of three or four residents and three or four students, in which they can play cards or other games, talk about various issues, and so on.

🍎 TEEN PAGES

Helene Perry is the homeroom teacher of students in grades 7 and 8 (Clara Barton Open School, in Minneapolis, is K–8). She has them for an hour a day and 90 minutes on Fridays. They put out a magazine, *Teen Pages*, about four times a year.

Beyond the fact that the magazine is interesting and informs its readership, this activity succeeds on a number of levels. Parents say that it's great to hear what the students are thinking. The students themselves improve their writing skills, especially because they're writing about things they care about. The students also learn the difference between fact and opinion, they learn to do graphics and tables, and they care about the content—they continually talk with one another about different articles. Teachers like it, too, and comment on the academic improvements they see in the students who help produce the magazine.

Ingredients

Time to write articles
Equipment and materials to put together a magazine, for example, a binding machine

Instructions

1 Brainstorm a theme for the current issue of the magazine, for example:

▶ "Leadership and Decision Making"
▶ "Caring and Sharing"
▶ "Sheroes and Heroes"
▶ "Peace, Love, and Harmony"

2 Brainstorm ideas in different categories, for example:

▶ Relationships
▶ Finance
▶ Technology
▶ Spirituality
▶ Health and fitness

Make a rule that students can't write in the same category twice in a row.

3 Have students submit their ideas for articles, and reassign topics if necessary so that every student is writing a different article.

4 Establish the criteria for the articles, including that they have to be at least a printed page, plus graphics; and that they have to include some research, for example, a survey, or information from a book.

5 Provide the use of computers in class.

6 Ask each student to submit at least two drafts.

7 Pair students, and have them read their articles to each other and give feedback.

8 Select one student from the class to design the cover of the current issue of the magazine and another student to write the introductory article.

9 Select editors, and have them put all the sheets together, make copies, and bind them.

10 Distribute the magazines to students and teachers.

Chef

Helene Perry, *teacher,* Clara Barton Open School, 4237 Colfax Avenue South, Minneapolis, MN 55409, 612-668-3580

Nutrients

#22—School engagement, #32—Planning and decision making, #30—Responsibility

Serves

75 students, grades 7–8

Variations

▶ You can have regular features in the magazine, for example:

- An editorial
- A cartoon strip
- A profile of a student who has done something special
- A call to action
- A crossword

▶ You can sell the magazine at PTA meetings, with the proceeds going toward some student or school function.

♥ X-TEND

The "TEND" in X-TEND stands for Teens Encouraging New Direction. It comes out of Lake Orion High School ("Orion" rhymes with "valedictorian"), Lake Orion, Michigan, and it's student-created and -driven. As school-to-careers coordinator Gloria Smith says, "If it's not student-driven, it's not going to work." The idea behind X-TEND is that middle school students—particularly those with problems—are much more likely to listen to high school students who themselves may have addressed those problems than to adults. The program is open to anyone, but up to this point it has focused on students who need the mentoring most.

Smith says that the program has succeeded in many ways, not the least of which is that the middle school students line up excitedly to get on the bus to the high school, and that they feel special when they get there. The high school students feel valuable, too—in the planning they do for the mentoring day, in the actual mentoring, and in the relationships they forge.

Ingredients

Surveys of students' interests
Transportation from the middle school(s) to the
  high school
A place to meet
Snacks

Instructions

1 Identify students in middle school—mostly through their teachers—who need help in doing homework, improving grades, and in general succeeding in school.

2 Identify students in high school who want to act as mentors and who may have had experiences similar to those of the middle school students.

3 Train the high school students in mentoring, for example, how to handle disclosures and how to establish boundaries.

4 Give each group of students surveys about their interests, skills, and experiences (e.g., music, sports, family situation), and pair them based on similarities.

5 Contract with each group of students for the mentorship.

6 Once a week, at 3:00 or just after school, pick up the middle school students and bring them over to the high school, where adults can monitor the mentoring.

7 Provide the following agenda:
▶ Snacks
▶ Homework
▶ Fun, asset-based activity for the whole group (planned by the high school students)
▶ Discussion of activity between student and mentor
▶ Discussion of activity with whole group

8 Arrange for students to be picked up at 5:00 or 5:30.

9 Continue this throughout the year.

Chef

Gloria Smith, *school-to-careers coordinator,* Lake Orion Schools, and Orion/Oxford Coalition—Asset Chair, 455 East Scripps Road, Lake Orion, MI 48360, 248-693-5675, gsmith@lakeorion.k12.mi.us

Nutrients

#23—Homework, #15—Positive peer influence, #9—Service to others

Serves

30 students, grades 6–12

Variations

▶ You can drop this activity down one whole level, so that middle school students mentor elementary school students.

▶ You can identify students who are doing especially well and set up a mentoring program that gives them more opportunities to explore their class work in greater depth.

Desserts

DESSERTS are asset-building activities that are fun, satisfying, and of little risk. They're the kinds of activities that people like to do because they're not strongly tied to a particular academic program or discipline and yet seem to make everyone connected with them feel good. These activities are similar to appetizers in that they're useful for schools that don't want to make big commitments to an activity, but they differ in that they're not deliberately used as a catalyst for additional asset-building activities.

☺ ADOPT-A-PARK

Beaver, Pennsylvania, is a 200-year-old town that has pre-served 10 parks in one square mile. People meet monthly from April through October to maintain their adopted park. The Borough of Beaver supplies the necessary tools, and the citizens provide the work, for example, weeding flower beds and making sure that the park provides safe playing areas for children. This year, people will erect signs that give credit to contributing clubs and organizations (e.g., "Gypsy Glen Park has been adopted by Beaver Area High School teachers and members of the Environmental Club").

Adopt-a-Park originated with high school clubs such as the Environmental Club and is now a partnership between Assets among Us (the local Healthy Communities • Healthy Youth initiative) and the borough, which is one of the communities located in the Beaver Area School District. The program has proved beneficial in several ways: Not only do parks receive some needed work, but students and adults work together, students are able to show that they can assume responsibility, and everyone has a chance to learn more about gardening and the environment.

Ingredients

Gardening equipment
Liaison with a representative from the local parks department or other appropriate agency
Student and staff volunteers

Instructions

1 Assess the needs of parks in your community for beautification and maintenance.

2 Publicize the needs in the school and solicit volunteers to help.

3 Work with representatives from the parks department or other appropriate agency to specify the tasks that need to be accomplished.

4 Choose a Saturday when school adults and students can work at the park.

5 Have school adults work with students to allocate tasks (e.g., weeding and planting) and to complete them.

6 Have a master gardener or other professionals on hand to give students information and guidance.

Chef

Ruth Briceland, *community coordinator,* Beaver Area School District, 855 2nd Street, Beaver, PA 15009, 724-774-9126, x230, briceland@basd.k12.pa.us

Nutrients

#9—Service to others, #8—Youth as resources, #10—Safety

Serves

20–35 students, grades 7–12

Variations

▶ You can coordinate the volunteer work with class work, for example, by conducting examinations of the needs of different kinds of plants; in fact, this activity works very well with only one classroom at a time.

▶ You can have students invite family members to participate.

 **See EXTRA HELPINGS**

► **Application to Adopt a Park** ◄

1. Name of individual, group, or organization _____

2. Contact person _____

3. Number of possible participants _____

4. Address _____

5. Phone _____ E-mail _____

6. Park you would like to adopt (please identify three parks with numbers 1, 2, and 3 as your first, second, and third choices)

_____ Irving Park (gazebo)	_____ Quay Square (bandstand)
_____ McIntosh Park (war monument)	_____ Bouquet Park
_____ Wayne Square	_____ Clark Park
_____ Linn Park	_____ Roosevelt Park (water lot)
_____ Gypsy Glen Park (high school)	_____ River Front Park

7. Would you be willing to work/share the above-mentioned park with another group or organization? _____

8. Would you or your group/organization be willing to (check all that apply):

_____ work once a month in park	_____ pick up branches
_____ plant trees	_____ pull weeds
_____ plant flowers	_____ inspect playground equipment
_____ inspect benches	_____ rake leaves
_____ paint benches or equipment	_____ plant grass
_____ edge sidewalks	_____ donate funds for planting

9. Would you or one member from your organization be willing to sit on an advisory committee? _____

⭐ ENSURING TOMORROW

Sue Sisley is a physician in Scottsdale, Arizona, who decided several years ago to do something with young people for young people. She collaborated with a local theater company, Desert Stages Theater, to bring young people together for the purpose of creating and staging a musical play about the consequences of teenage sex. The half-hour play is called *Think It Through Revue,* and it focuses on three couples who make different choices about sexual activity.

Since then, the group has added *Tobacco—The Musical* to their repertoire and is soon to complete a third musical play, this one about violence. The group goes on tour to schools, conferences, and recently to Disney World, where they perform free before young people and convey their message in a way that entertains as well as educates. They perform about four days a month, with about three shows a day.

"The medium of live musical theater is very engaging," says Sisley. It's engaging to the performers as well; most of the young people in the shows—volunteers all—have been with her from the beginning. Her collaboration with writer-composer Gerry Cullity and her liaison with not only schools but also medical organizations have resulted in a high-quality product being staged for numerous audiences around the state and throughout the country.

Ingredients

Liaison with an organization that can audition and
   coordinate talent
Coordination with schools

Instructions

1 Establish a liaison with a musical theater company or similar organization that's able to audition and coordinate talent.

2 Recruit students of all ages who can sing, dance, and act, and who are succeeding academically (stu-

dents on tour will inevitably miss some days of school).

3 Work with the students to formulate a treatment of an issue, and then give it to a writer-composer to enhance the dialogue and songs.

4 Conduct auditions for each role, select the players, and direct rehearsals.

5 Prerecord music, and arrange lighting, sets, and costumes.

6 Coordinate with schools to give free performances.

7 Set up advertising with local media to publicize the shows.

Chef

Sue Sisley, *president/CEO,* Ensuring Tomorrow Productions, 12622 North 81st Street, Scottsdale, AZ 85260, 888-780-6422, suesisley@aol.com, www.bannerhealthaz.com/ ensuringtomorrow.html

Nutrients

#31—Restraint, #17—Creative activities, #35—Resistance skills

Serves

40 students, grades 3–12 (14 in any one show)

Variations

▶ An effort like this one can be accomplished solely within a school setting; you can work with the music or theater teachers to stage a show and go on tour. Depending on your budget, the tours can range from your local area to the entire country. You can solicit sponsors to pay for costumes, advertising, transportation, staffing, and other expenses.

▶ You can arrange to make the presentations coincide with schools' focus on the specific topic of the show (i.e., sexuality or tobacco), and thus work it into the schools' curricula.

 EXTRA HELPINGS for *Ensuring Tomorrow: Lyrics from the* Think It Through Revue.

▶ *Excerpt from* **Think It Through Revue** ◀

Be sure of your choice . . . or it ain't worth it
Hold up your head and let the world see
Let your heart have a voice or it ain't worth it
It ain't worth the pain . . . that's a guarantee

Nothing comes easy, and nothing comes free
Your choice is what you pay
Living day to day
Needs you have to weigh
Scenes you can't replay
See, each decision is filled with a vision
Your life as it could be . . . fine and fancy-free
Worlds for you to see . . . no apology

Don't risk your life . . . it ain't worth it
Don't risk your love with the things that you choose
Give of your heart but keep your eyes wide open
You know it ain't worth it; there's a lot you can lose

☺ FIRST TEACHER

This activity is called First Teacher because a parent *is* a child's first teacher. It promotes asset #25—Reading for pleasure, but presumably it will take a while for the asset to manifest itself. Kathy Bottone and two other teachers organized their 4th- and 5th-grade classes to raise $140 to purchase books for mothers-to-be. More important, students wrote in their own words why it was important to read to babies and young children. The reasons ranged from the emotional ("It feels good to have someone read to you when you're a kid") to the practical ("You do better in school when you know how to read").

Ingredients

> Liaisons between school, hospital, and bookstore
> Data about local illiteracy rates

Instructions

1 Get support from the principal and the Parent Teacher Association.

2 Explain the project to a local bookstore and ask for discounts on books for babies and young children.

3 Gain access to the maternity ward of a local hospital and explain the project.

4 Ask students to raise money to purchase books for new mothers (e.g., *Goodnight, Moon* or *The Velveteen Rabbit*); suggest that they earn the money, not ask for it, by, for example:
▶ Doing chores around the house
▶ Doing chores around the neighborhood
▶ Giving up treats for lunch and donating the money
▶ Donating birthday money

5 Enlist students' help in purchasing books for mothers-to-be.

A cover drawing and the letter inside offer congratulations to new parents and encourage them to read to their new baby.

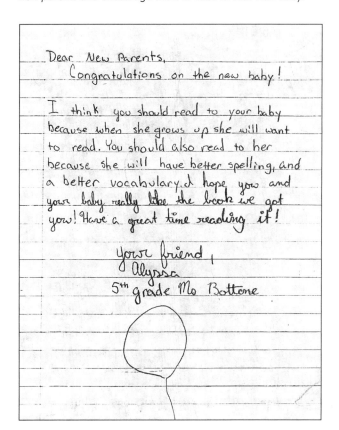

6 Discuss with students the reasons it's important to read to children, and have them write letters to the mothers-to-be stating those reasons. Augment the discussion with data about local illiteracy rates.

7 Wrap the books and enclose the letters.

8 Choose students to present the books and letters to the hospital.

9 Help students make a presentation about the project to the PTA.

Chef

Kathy Bottone, *teacher,* Drum Point Road School, 41 Drum Point Road, Brick, NJ 08723, 732-262-2570, kaat26@yahoo.com

Nutrients

#25—Reading for pleasure, #30—Responsibility, #15—Positive peer influence

Serves

25 families per month

Variations

▶ You can expand this activity to all grade levels. If you live in a lightly populated community, you can select other communities.

▶ You can ask students to read or to write books for the babies.

THE GREAT EPHEMERAL ART PROJECT

"It was phenomenal," says Gibson Elementary School art specialist Rebecca Gray. And so it was. Picture a figure of a child, clad in blue jeans, white shirt, and black shoes, with a big red heart on his chest. Picture this figure 100 feet tall, stretched out in the middle of a two-acre lot next to a school. Picture this figure made entirely of clothing, with the school name spelled in cans of Campbell's soup. Finally, picture this figure being completely disassembled and the clothing going to neighborhood charities.

This activity combines some powerful qualities: working together toward a common goal; learning about something new; caring for the less fortunate; and creating a huge work of art that's probably unlike anything any of the students have ever done and most have ever heard about. Gray said she was utterly unprepared for the emotion accompanying the culmination of the art project. Part of that emotion, no doubt, was a result of the sheer size of the project; but another part was a reflection of the children doing what they had previously thought was impossible.

Who worked on this project? Gray and her K–5 students were the primary creators—determining the theme, planning, measuring, collecting and sorting 24,903 articles of clothing (and almost 600 cans of soup, later donated to a food shelf), laying down the outline, filling in the outline, and then distributing the donated clothes. The project took about two months in all; the actual construction took three days. The experience will undoubtedly last a lifetime for everyone who took part in it.

Ingredients

Donated clothing
Donated soup cans
Gypsum
Twine
Use of a helicopter or airplane
Bags or other containers for clothing

An aerial view of the large-scale artwork created with donated used clothing by students and staff of Gibson Elementary School.

Instructions

1 Arrange for use of a large enough space for the project, for example, a playing field or any land near a school that can be temporarily secured from the local parks and recreation department.

2 Plan the project with students:
- ▶ The design
- ▶ The colors
- ▶ The size
- ▶ The measurements

3 Enlist the cooperation of the community to collect clean clothing—used as well as new—and cans of soup.

4 Sort the clothing by color when it comes in; have it deposited in a location at the school.

5 Take students out on the field to measure and plan where the parts of the figure will go; use string to mark the boundaries initially, and then cover the string with gypsum (to mark the outline), which can be donated.

6 According to the color scheme, begin laying out the clothes:

- ▶ Begin in the center of the figure and work outward.
- ▶ Arrange for classes to come out at assigned times to contribute to the artwork.
- ▶ Solicit parents to take groups of about 10 students to work on different parts of the figure.
- ▶ Use playground equipment, ladders, and other means to get a vantage point.

7 When the figure is completed, use multicolored clothing to form a background.

8 Use the soup cans to spell out the school name, title of the figure, or other message.

9 Invite people from the community for a ceremony.

10 Have students sit around the perimeter of the artwork and arrange for someone to take photographs from the air, for example, a television weather or traffic reporter.

11 Pick up the clothing, and sort it into children's, men's, and women's clothing, depending on the needs of the charities in the community.

12 Donate all the clothing.

13 Follow up the project by asking students to write or draw about their experience.

Chef

Rebecca Gray, *art specialist,* James I. Gibson Elementary School, Henderson, NV 89014, 702-799-8730, grayturf@aol.com

Nutrients

#22—School engagement, #17—Creative activities, #26—Caring

Serves

750 students, grades K–5

Variations

- ▶ You can obviously do this at any grade level and with many different media. Consider boxes or cans of other foods as a substitute for clothing.
- ▶ You can consider a variety of locations as well (e.g., rooftops, long, thin stretches of land, or the area surrounding a school). You could even take it citywide or countywide.

INNER-CITY BALLET

Madeline Lopez is a self-professed "loudmouth parent." What she means is that she's a concerned parent, and Lopez was definitely concerned with the lack of arts activities at her daughter's school, Thomas Hooker Elementary School in Bridgeport, Connecticut. There was a basic music class and a basic art class, but nothing that Lopez thought would stimulate students to reach beyond their perceived limits. So she did some research—on the Internet, with community agencies such as parks and recreation, with the school's principal. She helped to establish a Youth as Resources chapter in her school to coordinate the activities, she got a utility company—United Illuminating—to donate money, and she sent out flyers to gather support for various arts programs.

One of the programs is a partnership with the Stamford Ballet Company. The company agreed to give ballet lessons to students at Thomas Hooker for a reduced group rate of $60 per lesson. Lopez sent out flyers to all 1st-grade students and their parents; 11 girls signed up. Some of the changes over the course of the 10-week lessons were remarkable. "One girl," says Lopez, "just blossomed"—never missed a lesson, increased her self-esteem, improved her grades, and discovered a love for dance. Two other students had been failing as well as having poor attendance; next month they'll be on the honor roll.

Lopez learned a few lessons in this, her first formal attempt at coordinating school programs. "It's very difficult," she cautions. "Expect to be disappointed." On the other hand, she was thrilled at the support she received from other parents, from school staff—all of whom have contributed in one way or another—and from community agencies who are more than willing to donate money in exchange for favorable publicity. But Lopez has gotten the most satisfaction from seeing the benefits to the children. It's critical, she says, to "catch them while they're young."

Ingredients

Liaison with a community organization, such as a ballet company

Sponsorship from neighborhood agencies

Publicity for the program

Leotards or other dancing outfits for participating students

Instructions

1 Work with students to determine the feasibility of an after-school activity focusing on the arts.

2 Solicit support from an appropriate professional organization.

3 Send out flyers to both students and parents that describe the activity and the benefits to students.

4 Coordinate the activity; for example, set a time and place after school and arrange for transportation if necessary.

Chef

Madeline Lopez, 139 East Pasadena Place, Bridgeport, CT 06610, 203-372-5512

Nutrients

#17—Creative activities, #18—Youth programs, #38—Self-esteem

Serves

11 students, grade 1

Variations

▶ This is a structure for setting up a variety of after-school activities: Enlist support from students, administrators, staff, parents, and neighborhood agencies; and coordinate the activities. The keys are the support and the coordination.

▶ You can have students contribute to sustaining the activities. For example, videotape students participating in the activities or testifying to the benefits of the activities. Then you can use the video to enlist support from other organizations, students, administrators, staff, parents, and neighborhood agencies.

THE INTERGENERATIONAL POST-PROM PARTY

This is a wonderful idea that started in 1994, at Willow Lake High School; now, however, it's done all over South Dakota. Many students are amazed that the issues they currently address are similar to the ones the seniors addressed 50–60 years ago. The seniors often act as mentors for the students, and the relationships continue beyond the party.

Ingredients

An auditorium, gymnasium, or similar space
Access to senior groups (e.g., in nursing homes or
    through senior centers)
Round tables with tablecloths
Utensils
Decorations and refreshments
Music from the 1940s or other appropriate era
Corsages, boutonnieres, and name tags
Wheelchairs, walkers, stools with wheels
A Polaroid camera, film, and picture frames

Instructions

1 Reserve an auditorium or similar space for an appropriate time, for example, the day after the high school prom, in April or May, from about 2:00 to 4:00 on a Sunday afternoon.

2 Contact senior groups in the area and select a group to invite to the party.

3 Have students interview the seniors and conduct research on the Internet and at music stores to get CDs with music from when the seniors were young (e.g., the 1940s).

4 Have students discuss seniors' dietary needs with nutrition experts at the centers or nursing homes in order to plan what foods to serve at the party (e.g., punch and finger food).

5 Create and have seniors sign a dance card, which promises them dances with students. (You'll probably need to introduce students to the idea of a dance card first.)

6 Secure round tables with tablecloths, and arrange refreshments and decorations.

7 When the seniors get to the hall, present them with either a corsage or boutonniere and a name tag. Escort them to their table, perhaps several seniors and six or seven teenagers to a table. Appoint one student to preside over the table, for example, by introducing everyone.

8 Give teenagers printouts of the seniors who have signed dance cards; it's their responsibility to tap the seniors on the shoulder and ask them to dance.

9 Because the seniors sometimes use wheelchairs or walkers, have similar equipment available (e.g., stools on wheels) for the students to use when they dance.

10 Provide enough time for students to get acquainted with the seniors and ask them questions about their lives in the past—food, clothing, politics, social issues—and compare how things were then with how they are now.

11 Take photographs during the party, and provide them in frames for the seniors and students.

Chef

Gerry Likness, *agency resource manager,* Lutheran Brotherhood, 4113 12th Avenue NE, Watertown, SD 57201, 800-882-5983

Nutrients

#40—Positive view of personal future, #3—Other adult relationships, #33—Interpersonal competence

Serves

50 students, grades 9–12

Variations

▶ This activity typically occurs with high school students, but you can probably do something comparable with students as low as grade 6, pairing students with seniors of similar interests.

▶ You can hold the party during the winter holiday season instead of after the prom, add games or other forms of entertainment, and even videotape the event.

KNOWING THE COMMUNITY

This project was originally undertaken in 1991, when Sue Kidd facilitated a semester-long class in community research that was open to all 10th to 12th graders at Wamego High School in Wamego, Kansas. Students had to write a letter applying to take the course; 12 were chosen. The rest is not merely history but also the preservation of history.

An activity like this is rare: Not only did students get a valuable and memorable experience, not only did they use both left-brain planning and right-brain creativity, not only did they become fully engaged in learning, but they can point to their contribution every day. The markers still stand; the video still exists. They continue to affect people, years after the activity was completed. Such longevity is a wonderful testament to giving students the message that they can make a difference—now and in the future.

Ingredients

> *Videocassette recorder and other video-making equipment*
> *Materials with which to make historical markers*
> *Information about your community*
> *Permission from appropriate agencies*

Instructions

1 Research the history of your community, including the founders. Compare the leadership of the founders with contemporary leaders, and invite those contemporary leaders to speak with students.

2 Determine ways to make the community known to its citizens as well as visitors.

3 Develop an 8- to 10-minute video for the Chamber of Commerce that would attract families as much as businesses. Interview people, videotape street scenes, and work on the fades, credits, music, and everything else that goes into an effective video.

4 Make up a walking-biking-driving tour of the community, perhaps one to five miles long—showing historical landmarks, old houses and other buildings, and so on.

5 Get permission as necessary from the appropriate municipal and county agencies. Then solicit help from a high school metalworking class to make markers, which can then be affixed to the buildings. Request help from a high school woodworking class to make a kiosk that describes the tour, and install it at an appropriate location.

6 Solicit donations from the Chamber of Commerce to develop brochures publicizing the trail; distribute the brochures at local festivals and businesses.

Chef

Sue Kidd, 16879 46th Street, McLouth, KS 66054, 785-863-3425, suekidd@ruralnet1.com

Nutrients

#22—School engagement, #32—Planning and decision making, #17—Creative activities

Serves

12 students, grades 10–12

Variations

▶ You can have students make guides for specific populations in your community, for example, parents, visitors, the elderly, the disabled, and teenagers.
▶ You can have students give walking tours of your community.

THE MOM-DAD-ME CONCERT

Now in its fourth year, the Mom-Dad-Me concert features several hundred musicians from different generations, playing together in a way to delight the Livonia, New York, community. Douglas Hawk already had 90 students in his 5th-grade band and 69 students in his 6th-grade band; he combined them and added relatives, creating the formula for an annual concert. The concert has reaped many benefits: Parents have enjoyed the opportunity of "getting out the instrument again," and in some cases students have taken on the role of teacher to reeducate their parents. Another benefit is that students have had the opportunity to hear their parents play and sit next to them. Finally, the concert has been an incentive for younger students to continue to play, because they've been inspired by the others and have heard how well they might play in the future. Most of the parents have continued to return to play in the concert.

Ingredients

> Musical instruments and music
> Publicity
> A seating chart
> Time and place for rehearsals and performances

Instructions

1 Send letters home with band students inviting any parents, older siblings, or other relatives who can play instruments to join the band for a concert.

2 Arrange with local music stores to lend instruments at no cost for the concert.

3 Send home the music to any interested family members, along with the instruments.

4 Rehearse at school every day; invite the relatives, as well as any teachers who want to join, to the rehearsals.

5 Make up a seating chart, trying to get students sitting with their relatives, if possible, for example, by placing oboes with flutes or similar instruments.

6 Publicize the concert in the community, and hold it the last week of school.

Chef

Douglas Hawk, *music teacher,* Livonia Intermediate School, P.O. Box E, Livonia, NY 14487, 716-346-4030

Nutrients

#17—Creative activities, #21—Achievement motivation, #6—Parent involvement in schooling

Serves

150–200 students, grades 5–6

Variations

▶ You can have a Mom-Dad-Me concert for virtually any age-group, and you can hold it at any special occasion. You can even videotape it.

▶ You can ask relatives who play instruments to help tutor the band students or hold a special concert featuring just the relatives. Another option is to open up the band to anyone in the community who plays an instrument. You can even expand your concept of "instrument" to include, say, a variety of percussion (e.g., pots and pans) and wind (e.g., soda bottles) instruments.

READING IN THE PARK

This activity began with a Make a Difference Day grant awarded to the Foster Grandparent Program in Knoxville, Tennessee. Carolyn Walls, manager of the program, said that she and other coordinators carried out a two-pronged approach: soliciting volunteers to read to children, and publicizing the event to elementary school students through posters, letters to parents, visits to schools, and so on. Walls said that next time she'll cast a larger net to bring in students—about 70 came—but that the event was nonetheless a rousing success, both for the students and for the adults who volunteered.

This activity, I believe, might come under the heading of "making the medicine taste good." To those of us who read for pleasure, it seems almost inconceivable that someone would have to be persuaded to do so. Nonetheless, many young people do not have this developmental asset. Reading in the Park provides an optimum environment for young people of a range of abilities and interests to build this asset: The climate is comfortable, friendly, nonthreatening, and—perhaps most important—fun.

Ingredients

> A place to hold the event
> Coordination of the event among volunteers
> Lunches
> Enough books at a variety of reading levels for each
> student to take one home

Instructions

1 Solicit volunteers from community agencies to bring their favorite books to read to young people and to serve lunch.

2 Plan a four-hour event for a Saturday afternoon at a local park; get permission if necessary.

3 Purchase or otherwise secure enough books for every student to take one home.

4 Publicize the event at local elementary schools and youth-serving organizations.

5 Provide lunch, snacks, and beverages, as well as other entertainment (e.g., face painting).

6 On the day of the event, place books on tables sorted by age-groups and allow each student to take a book home.

7 Give students opportunities to join groups that are read to by volunteers; rotate the groups so that all young people get a variety of books read to them. Enlist parents who bring their children to volunteer as well.

Chef

Carolyn Walls, *manager,* Foster Grandparent Program, P.O. Box 51650, Knoxville, TN 37950, 865-524-2786, cwalls@knxcac.org

Nutrients

#25—Reading for pleasure, #4—Caring neighborhood, #13—Neighborhood boundaries

Serves

70 students, grades K–6

Variations

▶ You can enlist middle school, junior high school, or high school students to be the volunteer readers.

▶ You can coordinate the event with schools so that students who get free books read them and report to their classrooms on them.

SCHOOL CONNECTION

This is an interesting twist on the students-visit-jobs activity. In this activity, community people visit the students. Instead of students finding out what jobs are like, community people find out what school is like. The result is sometimes the beginning of good relationships and other times even employment for the students, but always interesting feedback and good public relations.

Ingredients

A committee to identify groups of community people
Cooperation of the school for a half day on each day of
the visit

A Camas school board member grins as he "shadows" a student to his algebra class.

Instructions

1 Identify groups of community members (e.g., seniors or businesspeople) who would be interested in being invited to spend some time with students in school.

2 Select the people, pair them with students, and invite them to the event.

3 Set aside a midweek morning for each visit.

4 At the beginning of the school day, have the volunteers meet with their student partners in the library, take refreshments, and attend the first three periods together—adult with student. Encourage the adults to participate in every activity with the student.

5 After that, convene the group without the students but with the principal and other staff. Provide lunch for the adults and solicit feedback about the morning.

Chef

Milt Dennison, *superintendent,* Camas School District, 2041 N.E. Ione, Camas, WA 98607, 360-817-4400

Nutrients

#7—Community values youth, #14—Adult role models, #21—Achievement motivation

Serves

100 students, grades 10–12

Variations

▶ You can include students in all the meetings, especially the ones in which the adults give feedback.

▶ You can coordinate class work with the group that's chosen (e.g., businesspeople, scientists, health professionals, or educators).

SHARING SENIORS

For 12 years, twice every year, Barbara Matthews brought in a panel of elderly people to speak to her family and consumer studies/health class, which had about 30 students. Students were shy about asking questions at first, but soon they were asking questions about what school had been like for the seniors and discussing topics such as sex and dying (Matthews remembers one student asking an Episcopal priest if he lusted in his heart after other women). The seniors could ask questions, too, like why a student had pierced body parts or purple hair. The class was at first 47 minutes, but Matthews eventually expanded it into lunch. When she found that students were fighting to sit near the seniors, she had to rotate tables. At the end of the school year, students invariably cited this as their favorite activity—even more than a sex education class.

Ingredients

A panel of seniors
Lunch or brunch supplies

Instructions

1 Solicit seniors from the local RSVP (Retired Seniors Volunteer Program) to talk with students; include a diversity of professions, cultures, and so on.

2 Ask the panelists to come in and give five-minute synopses of their lives, after which students can ask questions that they've prepared beforehand.

3 Be sure that the seniors know they have a right not to answer, and that everyone understands that the questions must be in good taste.

4 Give the seniors opportunities to ask questions of the students, too.

5 Extend the activity through lunch.

6 Discuss the activity with students the following day.

Chef

Barbara Matthews, *family consumer studies instructor (retired)*, Roseburg High School, P.O. Box 92, Riddle, OR 97469, 541-874-2409

Nutrients

#3—Other adult relationships, #33—Interpersonal competence, #40—Positive view of personal future

Serves

Students, grades 10–12

Variations

▶ You can have students visit seniors at a nursing home and conduct virtually the same activity.

▶ You can encourage seniors to visit your class throughout the year and offer their insight and experience on specific topics (e.g., science, drug education, politics, or history). Then you can incorporate that information into class work, for example, to determine trends or to gain perspective.

THE SKATEBOARD PARK

This activity is the prototype for many initiatives: You determine needs, bring interested students together, organize a plan, gather support, and implement the plan. In this case, because of limited funding, students had to build the skateboard park out of wood; now, however, because of extensive use, the park will have to be refashioned out of metal. Everyone benefited from this project: the adults, who were amazed at the students' energy and talents (which countered their first impressions); and the students, who learned a lot in designing the park and who eventually got to use it. An activity like this is motivation for working with local Chambers of Commerce to regularly set aside "feeder" money for student projects. And what better way to show that a community values youth than for it to listen to their ideas and support their plans?

Ingredients

A place to meet
Building materials and funds
Volunteers from the community
Space for the park

Instructions

1 Call a meeting at the school and have the skateboarders identify themselves.

2 Work with the students to do the following:

▶ Identify a location for a skateboard park;

▶ Make plans for construction;

▶ Secure funding for materials (e.g., from the Chamber of Commerce);

▶ Acquire the materials;

▶ Make a presentation (e.g., at the Elks Club) to solicit assistance; and

▶ Over a few weekends, build it.

Chef

Suzanne Johnston, *coordinator*, Youth Plus, 105 West Adams, Suite B, Creston, IA 50801, 641-782-8426

Nutrients

#7—Community values youth, #32—Planning and decision making, #8—Youth as resources

Serves

Students, grades 10–12

Variations

▶ You can make connections with local businesses to tutor students in what they need to know in order to complete their project.

▶ You can team students with members of community service clubs.

☺ SWAT

Florida, like a number of other states, has received money —$13 billion so far—from settlements with tobacco companies; with this money, the state created a statewide organization called SWAT—Students Working Against Tobacco. SWAT has chapters in counties as well as schools; all students ages 12–18 who attend a Florida middle school or high school are eligible to participate. Students regularly receive training at conferences held throughout the year. They develop commercials, put out magazines, design materials, run a Web site, and in general advocate for a tobacco-free society.

Ingredients

> Access to resources about tobacco and tobacco use
> Trainers and advisers
> Funding commensurate with students' goals

Instructions

1 Organize students for the purpose of raising awareness about young people's tobacco use and the strategies of corporations to persuade them to use tobacco.

2 Train students in topics related to tobacco and tobacco use.

3 Have students meet weekly and discuss ways to promote awareness, for example:
- ▶ Establish liaisons with journalists and local legislators
- ▶ Make presentations
- ▶ Staff booths at fairs and other events
- ▶ Give out information via brochures, flyers, and newsletters
- ▶ Sell T-shirts, bumper stickers, buttons, key chains, hats, and other materials that promote their goals
- ▶ Develop posters and other advertising material

4 Give students opportunities to use other strategies to fight "Big Tobacco," for example, by working with police to surreptitiously determine whether stores sell tobacco to minors.

Chefs

Luisa Bigger, *college and career counselor,* Coral Shores High School, 89901 Old Highway, Tavernier, FL 33070, 305-853-3222, X316 (W), flgiraffelady@aol.com;
Tobacco Prevention and Control Office, Miami-Dade County Health Department, 1444 Biscayne Boulevard, Suite 302, Miami, FL 33132, 305-377-5010, www.wholetruth.com

Nutrients

#28—Integrity, #32—Planning and decision making, #35—Resistance skills

Serves

35 students, grades 9–12

Variations

- ▶ You can use SWAT-type activities to meet requirements of character education, service-learning, or independent or group projects.
- ▶ You can focus on any of the following issues, either in classrooms or communities:
  - The short- and long-term effects of tobacco use
  - Advertising techniques used by corporations
  - Corporate profits resulting from sales to minors, both in the United States and abroad
  - Secondhand smoke
  - Policies of businesses (e.g., restaurants) toward smoking
  - Cultural norms toward tobacco use
  - The influence of celebrity athletes on tobacco use
  - The dynamics of addiction

SWAT's Goals

from "Build It!," a guide produced
in 1999 by SWAT

- Provide a means for Florida's youth to develop and coordinate a unified assault on tobacco's sales pitch in their communities.
- Encourage youth to become effective advocates and leaders in their communities, regions, and state.
- Provide youth with "real-life" experiences through planning, executing, and evaluating tobacco prevention activities.
- Train youth to be more effective in all endeavors they choose to undertake.
- Work in tandem with adults within the Tobacco Pilot Program.

Top Tips for Giving Reporters What They Want

from "Hype It!," a guide produced in 1999 by SWAT

- Do your homework before approaching the media. Look at the type of events your local TV, radio, or newspapers usually run and then try to copy it.
- When planning an event, think carefully about the type of event or activity and ask yourself: Will this be interesting to the media?
- If in doubt about how interesting an event will be to the media, call a reporter (one who has covered a SWAT event in the past) and run your idea past her. First ask her if she can spare two minutes, then ask if she would be interested in covering it.
- Stories that feature good photo opportunities are always popular with print and TV reporters—consider how you can make your event as visual as possible.

THE TEEN DOCENT PROGRAM

This program began at the University of Oregon, and it reaches out to any middle or high school in the Eugene area. It could just as easily start in the middle or high school, however; the main connection is the liaison between the museum and the schools. The program is in its third year, and students benefit greatly not only from the knowledge they gain in the field of art but also from the experience of communicating with audiences. Even activities like The Teen Docent Program, which directly affect only a small number of students, can be extremely powerful. The interpersonal competence initially supported by this activity can last a lifetime.

Ingredients

Liaison between museum and schools
A training course

Instructions

1 Ask students interested in art and communications if any would like to become docents.

2 Coordinate with a local museum to set up training (e.g., two hours, once a week), which would include the following:
▶ Art history
▶ The psychology of audiences
▶ Teaching strategies
▶ Public speaking
▶ Evaluated "walk-throughs"
▶ Slides, discussions, and guest expert lectures
▶ Familiarization with the museum's permanent collection as well as temporary exhibitions

3 When training is completed, allow students to conduct tours in the museum.

4 Give students opportunities to use objects from the museum's education department to supplement their lectures at schools, nursing homes, and other places in the community.

Chef

Lisa Abia-Smith, *director of education,* University of Oregon, 1223 University of Oregon, Eugene, OR 97403, 541-346-0966, abiasmlm@oregon.uoregon.edu

Nutrients

#17—Creative activities, #33—Interpersonal competence, #22—School engagement

Serves

12 students per semester, grades 6–12

Variations

▶ You can have the docents give tours not only to the public but also to selected classrooms from their own schools.
▶ You can coordinate a docent program with another arts or sciences institution (e.g., theater, aquarium, planetarium, symphony).

September 12, 2000

Hi, Lisa and Deborah,

This is Elisha, and I just wanted to tell you about everything that has been happening to me in college [Pepperdine]. I applied for a part-time job with my work study at the on-campus museum called Frederick R. Weisman Museum. On the application I wrote about my experience at the U of O for two years in the teen docent program there, and the lady referred me to the director of the museum and the only staff! He gave me a job last week. The amazing thing is that he is wanting to start everything that I had been working on at the U of O, such as touring children, making outreach visits to low-income schools without art programs, and touring any kind of group through the museum. Since he does EVERYTHING, he also needed an assistant. I will be learning how to do everything, which I am excited [about], because this is an awesome experience. He rents the exhibits, calls and finds the art, makes the catalogs, writes the essays, paints the walls, sets the art up in the museum, etc.

A really exciting thing happened last night. The seniors here, studying to become teachers, were learning about how to teach art to children and were going to go to the school, introduce the artwork at the museum, and then the kids will visit the museum. So last night, I copied some touring techniques material for them and taught them how to tour children in an art museum! You don't know how many times I've heard "I love you" from these people here. The material that you've used has really helped them.

Thanks, Elisha

★ TEENS ON TOUR

This is a good example of an activity that combines several assets and keeps on building them as the young people participate in it. Donna Culotta-Kehler's 15-year-old daughter, Devon, had been involved in both music and volunteering for several years, when the two hit on an idea that seemed a natural: bring together some of Devon's friends who were also involved in music and "go on tour" to expose people—for example, people in nursing homes—to their art and talent.

And so they did. Devon was a participant in the Frederick County Advanced Musical Studies program, and so were some of her friends. They recruited several others, asking anyone under 16 to get parental permission, and Donna lined up a nursing home for a 45-minute performance. It was a huge success, and by now the group, Teens on Tour, has several weekend gigs in the works. The performers—including instrumentalists, vocalists, a ventriloquist, and a signer—love what they do, and the audiences do as well. The performances aren't scripted; each show depends on who's available and what they decide to do. But that just adds to the spontaneity, and it affords audiences a unique experience they probably would not otherwise have.

Ingredients

Volunteers who can perform
Coordination of events

Instructions

1 Bring together young people who are proficient in some aspect of performing, for example, actors, jugglers, instrumentalists, and vocalists.

2 Arrange performances in which they showcase their instrument or talent.

3 Coordinate free performances at nonprofit organizations and charities throughout the community.

4 Call on people to check on their accessibility several weeks before the performance, and keep the agenda flexible enough to accommodate a variety of performers.

Chefs

Devon Kehler and Donna Culotta-Kehler, 8654 Indian Springs Road, Frederick, MD 21702, 301-620-9515, thehill76@msn.com

Nutrients

#17—Creative activities, #26—Caring, #38—Self-esteem

Serves

At least 20 students, grades 7–12

Variations

▶ You can create performances for elementary-age students, introducing them to different instruments and different types of music.

▶ You can create demo tapes or CDs of some of the performances to send to prospective audiences in order to generate enthusiasm.

TIGER OF THE WEEK

While a school involvement coordinator charged with raising the spirits of Summit County High School—about 700 students—Jody Wilson conceived the idea of "Tiger of the Week." One girl, who'd failed almost everything as a junior but then made a comeback as a senior, was so thrilled that as she walked down the hall after being informed of her selection, she told everyone she saw, "I'm Tiger of the Week! I'm Tiger of the Week!"

One perhaps subtle factor of this activity is the role played by local businesses. By participating in this activity—and the participation can run the gamut from donating money to taking an active part in designing the ad to hosting an event in the student's honor—businesses enter into a partnership with the school that can take many forms in later activities. This partnership can reap benefits for the businesses, the school, and, most important, the students.

Ingredients

Support of local businesses and the local newspaper
School staff to choose a student each week

Instructions

1 Each week, ask a different member of the staff to select and write a few sentences about a student to be "(Mascot) of the Week"—a student who has generally been unrecognized.

2 Solicit businesses to sponsor the "(Mascot) of the Week" by purchasing space in the local newspaper.

3 Each week, have the reporter come to the school, take a photograph of the "(Mascot) of the Week," and gather information for the article.

4 Take the student out of class, read what the staff person wrote, and then ask the student to guess the identity of the writer.

5 Announce the "(Mascot) of the Week" throughout the school.

Chef

Jody Wilson, *counselor,* Summit County High School, P.O. Box 7, Frisco, CO 80443, 970-547-9311, X1194

Nutrients

#38—Self-esteem, #24—Bonding to school, #5—Caring school climate

Serves

700 students, grades 9–12

Variations

▶ You can set up specific criteria for the recognition (e.g., having done something selfless or having brought good publicity to the school) and have several staff people make nominations or have students nominate each other.

▶ You can have students fill out ballots for a "Staff Person of the Month."

VIDEO FOR ANIMALS

This is one of several activities Dannelly Elementary School does to help out the community. This particular activity started when a student wrote a story that involved, uncritically, a cruel act toward an animal. The incident spurred Terry Stanton and others to come up with an activity that had several goals: to teach students how to treat animals kindly; to encourage them to help their community; to get them familiar with all that goes into making a video; and to give them responsibility for creating, sequencing, and writing a public service announcement. Stanton is working primarily with 2nd-grade students in developing the videos.

Stanton cites an excellent reason for helping students learn how to care for others in the community: "One day, they'll *be* the community."

Ingredients

Video equipment
A partnership with a cable or television station
Liaison with an animal shelter

Instructions

1 Have someone from a local shelter (e.g., a branch of the Humane Society) bring in animals and show students how to treat them kindly.

2 Have students make posters illustrating the kind treatment of animals.

3 Consider having students (e.g., special ed. students) bring animals from the shelter to nursing homes and spend some time with elderly people and the animals.

4 Help students make videotapes about the kind treatment of animals, including:
▶ Brainstorming ideas for scripts
▶ Arranging the ideas sequentially
▶ Writing the script
▶ Determining how the video will be shot
▶ Shooting the video

5 Arrange with a local cable or television station to air the videotapes.

Chef

Terry Stanton, *technology coordinator,* Dannelly Elementary School, 3425 Carter Hill Road, Montgomery, AL 36111, 334-269-3657

Nutrients

#30—Responsibility, #17—Creative activities, #22—School engagement

Serves

Up to 500 students, grades K–5

Variations

▶ You can "adopt" pets from the shelter (appropriate for the classroom) and allocate responsibility for their care to students.
▶ You can have students assist representatives from the shelter in their presentations to other classrooms and schools.

Planning Your Meals

THE FOLLOWING lists and charts are intended to help you as you plan the "recipes" you want to use in creating a healthy menu of activities for and with the students in your school community.

Three Sample Menus

It's easy to put together menus of asset-building recipes: You assess the resources and circumstances of your school community, and you do what you can do. You might start out with an appetizer for that first flush of success, then continue with one or two side dishes. Once you've got a pretty good idea of the level of assets experienced by the young people in your school—say, after having administered and then interpreted the results of the *Search Institute Profiles of Student Life: Attitudes and Behaviors* survey—you might implement a main dish. And periodically, you might serve up a dessert as a reward for things done and an incentive for things yet to do.

Here are three menus, arranged by the type of recipe—just one way to construct a menu. If you want to focus, for example, on developing students' responsibility for helping others, you might take a look at this first menu. The appetizer, Making a Difference at School, is ideal for bringing a community together toward a common goal. Kids Helping Neighbors is a classroom activity, but you can implement it in virtually every classroom in your school. While that's going on, you can engage some of the seniors in your community in Seniors on the Internet. Finally, First Teacher gets at the rudiments of education while making everyone feel good about it.

The other two menus are similarly arranged. The second menu is appropriate for emphasizing learning, and the third for setting up asset-building structures in your school community. You should know by now, though, that this isn't by any means prescriptive. You may want to test the waters with merely an appetizer or two. You may be sufficiently confident to tackle a main course right away. Or you might be into it for the pleasure and confine yourself to a buffet of desserts. Whatever you do, try to make everything nutritious (addressing plenty of assets), well balanced (a variety of media and activities), and tasty (fun). Building assets, like a good meal, is often its own reward.

▶ **A Menu for** ◀
Service to Others

Appetizer
Making a Difference
at School

Main Course
Kids Helping Neighbors

Side Dish
Seniors on the Internet

Dessert
First Teacher

▶ **A Menu for** ◀
Learning

Appetizer
Bronco Choice 2000

Main Course
IMPACT

Side Dish
After-School
Homework Clubs

Dessert
Video for Animals

▶ **A Menu for** ◀
Setting up Asset-Building
Structures

Appetizer
The Wall of Assets

Main Course
A Community Taking
the Initiative

Side Dish
ASK

Dessert
School Connection

Recipes, by Area of School Life

From the perspective of the teacher and administrator, school life can be divided into five general areas:

- Curriculum and instruction (what's taught and how it's taught);
- Organization (the structure of the building and the school day);
- Cocurricular programs (after-school and before-school programs, or what used to be called "extracurricular" programs);
- Community partnerships (relationships with families, neighbors, volunteers, and community organizations and businesses); and
- Support services (health care, counseling).

Although the "recipes" in this book don't always fall neatly into just one area or another, the following chart should provide you with a general idea of where you might implement them in your school or district.

Area	Recipes	Page
CURRICULUM AND INSTRUCTION	Artists in Classrooms	71
	Kids in the Hall	83
	Math Buddies	90
	Teen Pages	107
	The HERO Program	79
	The Race, Culture, and Ethnicity Workshop	95
	Letters of Encouragement	21
	X-TEND	109
	Knowing the Community	126
	Business Links	75
	The Farm	45
	The Proud Panther	93
	The Mom-Dad-Me Concert	127
	SWAT	132
	Ensuring Tomorrow	115
	The Great Ephemeral Art Project	119
ORGANIZATION	The Dining Room	19
	The Wall of Assets	32

Recipes, by Asset

Each activity in this book addresses numerous assets. The following chart is organized by the top three assets built through each activity; therefore, you'll find each activity listed three times.

Asset		Recipes	Page
SUPPORT	1. Family support	Walk Your Child to School Day	31
	2. Positive family communication	The Alaska Game	11
		Walk Your Child to School Day	31
		CLUE	76
		Kids Helping Neighbors	49
	3. Other adult relationships	PALS	26
		The Farm	45
		After-School Homework Clubs	69
		Foster Grandparents	78
		Ministry to Neighborhood Children	92
		The Community Chest	40
		The Orion Program	54
		Save One Student	97
		Sharing Seniors	130
		The Dining Room	19
		Lunch Buddies	89
		The Intergenerational Post-Prom Party	124
		Bridge	73
	4. Caring neighborhood	The Alaska Game	11
		The Community Chest	40
		The Orion Program	54
		The Asset Banner Run-Walk-Crawl	13
		Making a Difference at School	24
		Reading in the Park	128
		Letters of Encouragement	21
	5. Caring school climate	Strengths in Families	60
		PALS	26

Asset		Recipes	Page
EMPOWERMENT (cont.)		Asset Ambassadors	37
		Steppin' Up to Solutions	58
		Adopt-a-Park	113
		Neighborhood Youth Councils	51
		The Reading Fair	28
	9. Service to others	X-TEND	109
		Adopt-a-Park	113
	10. Safety	Upstairs	63
		Play Fair	27
		Adopt-a-Park	113
BOUNDARIES & EXPECTATIONS	**11. Family boundaries**	Strengths in Families	60
		CLUE	76
	12. School boundaries	CLUE	76
		Kindness Chains	84
	13. Neighborhood boundaries	Learn to Earn	86
		Celebrate the Child Day	39
		The Asset Banner Run-Walk-Crawl	13
		Reading in the Park	128
	14. Adult role models	PALS	26
		The Dining Room	19
		Lunch Buddies	89
		Artists in Classrooms	71
		School Connection	129
	15. Positive peer influence	ASK	72
		IMPACT	48
		Asset Ambassadors	37
		X-TEND	109
		Assets from a Hat	15
		First Teacher	117
		READ	96

Asset		Recipes	Page
SOCIAL COMPETENCIES (cont.)	**35. Resistance skills**	Ensuring Tomorrow	115
		Bronco Choice 2000	16
		ASK	72
		IMPACT	48
		SWAT	132
	36. Peaceful conflict resolution	The Alaska Game	11
		The Race, Culture, and Ethnicity Workshop	95
		Anger Management?	70
POSITIVE IDENTITY	**37. Personal power**	Bronco Choice 2000	16
		A Community Taking the Initiative	41
		Steppin' Up to Solutions	58
		Upstairs	63
		Neighborhood Youth Councils	51
		The Wall of Assets	32
		Kids as Shoppers	81
		Strength Interviews	30
	38. Self-esteem	Tiger of the Week	137
		Teens on Tour	136
		Letters of Encouragement	21
		Inner-City Ballet	122
	39. Sense of purpose	Vocations On-Site	65
		Share a Friend	102
	40. Positive view of personal future	Vocations On-Site	65
		Sharing Seniors	130
		The Intergenerational Post-Prom Party	124
		Business Links	75
		The Wall of Assets	32
		Strength Interviews	30

Recipes, by State

Look at the following chart to find the activities of your state and other states in your region.

State	Recipe	Page
ALABAMA	Video for Animals	138
ALASKA	Strengths in Families	60
	The Alaska Game	11
ARIZONA	Ensuring Tomorrow	115
ARKANSAS	*The Proud Panther*	93
CALIFORNIA	PALS	26
	Bronco Choice 2000	16
	The Farm	45
COLORADO	Tiger of the Week	137
	Walk Your Child to School Day	31
	Learning to Volunteer	87
CONNECTICUT	Inner-City Ballet	122
DELAWARE	Vocations On-Site	65
FLORIDA	A Community Taking the Initiative	41
	Learn to Earn	86
	SWAT	132
GEORGIA	CLUE	76
HAWAII	School-Grown Vegetables	100
IDAHO	ASK	72
	After-School Homework Clubs	69
ILLINOIS	Share a Friend	102
INDIANA	Kids Helping Neighbors	49
IOWA	Seniors on the Internet	101
	The Skateboard Park	131
	IMPACT	48
KANSAS	Foster Grandparents	78
	Kids in the Hall	83
	Knowing the Community	126
KENTUCKY	Celebrate the Child Day	39
LOUISIANA	Ministry to Neighborhood Children	92
MAINE	Asset Ambassadors	37
	A 6th-Grade Yarn	103
MARYLAND	Teens on Tour	136
MASSACHUSETTS	The Race, Culture, and Ethnicity Workshop	95
MICHIGAN	The Family Resource Room	43
	X-TEND	109
MINNESOTA	*Teen Pages*	107

Search Institute has identified the following building blocks of healthy development that help young people grow up healthy, caring, and responsible.

EXTERNAL ASSETS

Support

1. **Family support**—Family life provides high levels of love and support.
2. **Positive family communication**—Young person and her or his parent(s) communicate positively, and young person is willing to seek advice and counsel from parents.
3. **Other adult relationships**—Young person receives support from three or more nonparent adults.
4. **Caring neighborhood**—Young person experiences caring neighbors.
5. **Caring school climate**—School provides a caring, encouraging environment.
6. **Parent involvement in schooling**—Parent(s) are actively involved in helping young person succeed in school.

Empowerment

7. **Community values youth**—Young person perceives that adults in the community value youth.
8. **Youth as resources**—Young people are given useful roles in the community.
9. **Service to others**—Young person serves in the community one hour or more per week.
10. **Safety**—Young person feels safe at home, at school, and in the neighborhood.

Boundaries and Expectations

11. **Family boundaries**—Family has clear rules and consequences and monitors the young person's whereabouts.
12. **School boundaries**—School provides clear rules and consequences.
13. **Neighborhood boundaries**—Neighbors take responsibility for monitoring young people's behavior.
14. **Adult role models**—Parent(s) and other adults model positive, responsible behavior.
15. **Positive peer influence**—Young person's best friends model responsible behavior.
16. **High expectations**—Both parent(s) and teachers encourage the young person to do well.

Constructive Use of Time

17. **Creative activities**—Young person spends three or more hours per week in lessons or practice in music, theater, or other arts.
18. **Youth programs**—Young person spends three or more hours per week in sports, clubs, or organizations at school and/or in the community.
19. **Religious community**—Young person spends one or more hours per week in activities in a religious institution.
20. **Time at home**—Young person is out with friends "with nothing special to do" two or fewer nights per week.

INTERNAL ASSETS

Commitment to Learning

21. **Achievement motivation**—Young person is motivated to do well in school.
22. **School engagement**—Young person is actively engaged in learning.
23. **Homework**—Young person reports doing at least one hour of homework every school day.
24. **Bonding to school**—Young person cares about her or his school.
25. **Reading for pleasure**—Young person reads for pleasure three or more hours per week.

Positive Values

26. **Caring**—Young person places high value on helping other people.
27. **Equality and social justice**—Young person places high value on promoting equality and reducing hunger and poverty.
28. **Integrity**—Young person acts on convictions and stands up for her or his beliefs.
29. **Honesty**—Young person "tells the truth even when it is not easy."
30. **Responsibility**—Young person accepts and takes personal responsibility.
31. **Restraint**—Young person believes it is important not to be sexually active or to use alcohol or other drugs.

Social Competencies

32. **Planning and decision making**—Young person knows how to plan ahead and make choices.
33. **Interpersonal competence**—Young person has empathy, sensitivity, and friendship skills.
34. **Cultural competence**—Young person has knowledge of and comfort with people of different cultural/racial/ethnic backgrounds.
35. **Resistance skills**—Young person can resist negative peer pressure and dangerous situations.
36. **Peaceful conflict resolution**—Young person seeks to resolve conflict nonviolently.

Positive Identity

37. **Personal power**—Young person feels he or she has control over "things that happen to me."
38. **Self-esteem**—Young person reports having a high self-esteem.
39. **Sense of purpose**—Young person reports that "my life has a purpose."
40. **Positive view of personal future**—Young person is optimistic about her or his personal future.

La investigación realizada por el Instituto Search ha identificado los siguientes elementos fundamentales del desarrollo como instrumentos para ayudar a los jóvenes a crecer sanos, interesados en el bienestar común y a ser responsables.

ELEMENTOS FUNDAMENTALES EXTERNOS

Apoyo

1. **Apoyo familiar**—La vida familiar brinda altos niveles de amor y apoyo.
2. **Comunicación familiar positiva**—El (La) joven y sus padres se comunican positivamente. Los jóvenes están dispuestos a buscar consejo y consuelo en sus padres.
3. **Otras relaciones con adultos**—Además de sus padres, los jóvenes reciben apoyo de tres o más personas adultas que no son sus parientes.
4. **Una comunidad comprometida**—El (La) joven experimenta el interés de sus vecinos por su bienestar.
5. **Un plantel educativo que se interesa por el (la) joven**—La escuela proporciona un ambiente que anima y se preocupa por la juventud.
6. **La participación de los padres en las actividades escolares**—Los padres participan activamente ayudando a los jóvenes a tener éxito en la escuela.

Fortalecimiento

7. **La comunidad valora a la juventud**—El (La) joven percibe que los adultos en la comunidad valoran a la juventud.
8. **La juventud como un recurso**—Se le brinda a los jóvenes la oportunidad de tomar un papel útil en la comunidad.
9. **Servicio a los demás**—La gente joven participa brindando servicios a su comunidad una hora o más a la semana.
10. **Seguridad**—Los jóvenes se sienten seguros en casa, en la escuela y en el vecindario.

Límites y expectativas

11. **Límites familiares**—La familia tiene reglas y consecuencias bien claras, además vigila las actividades de los jóvenes.
12. **Límites escolares**—En la escuela proporciona reglas y consecuencias bien claras.
13. **Límites vecinales**—Los vecinos asumen la responsabilidad de vigilar el comportamiento de los jóvenes.
14. **El comportamiento de los adultos como ejemplo**—Los padres y otros adultos tienen un comportamiento positivo y responsable.
15. **Compañeros como influencia positiva**—Los mejores amigos del (la) joven son un buen ejemplo de comportamiento responsable.
16. **Altas expectativas**—Ambos padres y maestros motivan a los jóvenes para que tengan éxito.

Uso constructivo del tiempo

17. **Actividades creativas**—Los jóvenes pasan tres horas o más a la semana en lecciones de música, teatro u otras artes.
18. **Programas juveniles**—Los jóvenes pasan tres horas o más a la semana practicando algún deporte, o en organizaciones en la escuela o de la comunidad.
19. **Comunidad religiosa**—Los jóvenes pasan una hora o más a la semana en actividades organizadas por alguna institución religiosa.
20. **Tiempo en casa**—Los jóvenes conviven con sus amigos "sin nada especial que hacer" dos o pocas noches por semana.

ELEMENTOS FUNDAMENTALES INTERNOS

Compromiso con el aprendizaje

21. **Motivación por sus logros**—El (La) joven es motivado(a) para que salga bien en la escuela.
22. **Compromiso con la escuela**—El (La) joven participa activamente con el aprendizaje.
23. **Tarea**—El (La) joven debe hacer su tarea escolar por lo menos durante una hora cada día de clases.
24. **Preocuparse por la escuela**—Al (A la) joven debe importarle su escuela.
25. **Leer por placer**—El (La) joven lee por placer tres horas o más por semana.

Valores positivos

26. **Preocuparse por los demás**—El (La) joven valora ayudar a los demás.
27. **Igualdad y justicia social**—Para el (la) joven tiene mucho valor el promover la igualdad y reducir el hambre y la pobreza.
28. **Integridad**—El (La) joven actúa con convicción y defiende sus creencias.
29. **Honestidad**—El (La) joven "dice la verdad aún cuando esto no sea fácil".
30. **Responsabilidad**—El (La) joven acepta y toma responsabilidad por su persona.
31. **Abstinencia**—El (La) joven cree que es importante no estar activo(a) sexualmente, ni usar alcohol u otras drogas.

Capacidad social

32. **Planeación y toma de decisiones**—El (La) joven sabe cómo planear y hacer elecciones.
33. **Capacidad interpersonal**—El (La) joven es simpático, sensible y hábil para hacer amistades.
34. **Capacidad cultural**—El (La) joven tiene conocimiento de y sabe convivir con gente de diferente marco cultural, racial o étnico.
35. **Habilidad de resistencia**—El (La) joven puede resistir la presión negativa de los compañeros así como las situaciones peligrosas.
36. **Solución pacífica de conflictos**—El (La) joven busca resolver los conflictos sin violencia.

Identidad positiva

37. **Poder personal**—El (La) joven siente que él o ella tiene el control de "las cosas que le suceden".
38. **Auto-estima**—El (La) joven afirma tener una alta autoestima.
39. **Sentido de propósito**—El (La) joven afirma que "mi vida tiene un propósito".
40. **Visión positiva del futuro personal**—El (La) joven es optimista sobre su futuro mismo.

Le Search Institute a défini les pierres angulaires suivantes qui aident les jeunes à devenir des personnes saines, bienveillantes et responsables.

ACQUIS EXTERNES

Soutien

1. **Soutien familial**—La vie familiale est caractérisée par un degré élevé d'amour et de soutien.
2. **Communication familiale positive**—Le jeune et ses parents communiquent positivement, et le jeune est disposé à leur demander conseil.
3. **Relations avec d'autres adultes**—Le jeune bénéficie de l'appui d'au moins trois adultes autres que ses parents.
4. **Voisinage bienveillant**—Le jeune a des voisins bienveillants.
5. **Milieu scolaire bienveillant**—L'école fournit au jeune un milieu bienveillant et encourageant.
6. **Engagement des parents dans les activités scolaires**—Les parents aident activement le jeune à réussir à l'école.

Prise en charge

7. **Valorisation des jeunes par la communauté**—Le jeune perçoit que les adultes dans la communauté accordent de l'importance aux jeunes.
8. **Rôle des jeunes en tant que ressources**—Le jeune se voit confier des rôles utiles dans la communauté.
9. **Service à son prochain**—Le jeune consacre à sa communauté au moins une heure par semaine.
10. **Sécurité**—Le jeune se sent en sécurité à la maison, à l'école et dans le quartier.

Limites et attentes

11. **Limites dans la famille**—La famille a des règlements clairs accompagnés de conséquences, et elle surveille les comportements du jeune.
12. **Limite à l'école**—L'école a des règlements clairs accompagnés de conséquences.
13. **Limites dans le quartier**—Les voisins assument la responsabilité de surveiller les comportements du jeune.
14. **Adultes servant de modèles**—Les parents et d'autres adultes dans l'entourage du jeune affichent un comportement positif et responsable.
15. **Influence positive des pairs**—Les meilleurs amis du jeune affichent un comportement responsable.
16. **Attentes élevées**—Les parents et les professeurs du jeune l'encouragent à réussir.

Utilisation constructive du temps

17. **Activités créatives**—Le jeune consacre au moins trois heures par semaine à suivre des cours de musique, de théâtre ou autres, et à mettre ses nouvelles connaissances en pratique.
18. **Programmes jeunesse**—Le jeune consacre au moins trois heures par semaine à des activités sportives, des clubs ou des associations à l'école et/ou dans la communauté.
19. **Communauté religieuse**—Le jeune consacre au moins trois heures par semaine à des activités dans une institution religieuse.
20. **Temps à la maison**—Le jeune sort avec des amis sans but particulier deux ou trois soirs par semaine.

ACQUIS INTERNES

Engagement envers l'apprentissage

21. **Encouragement à la réussite**—Le jeune est encouragé à réussir à l'école.
22. **Engagement à l'école**—Le jeune s'engage activement à apprendre.
23. **Devoirs**—Le jeune consacre au moins une heure par jour à ses devoirs.
24. **Appartenance à l'école**—Le jeune se préoccupe de son école.
25. **Plaisir de lire**—Le jeune lit pour son plaisir au moins trois heures par semaine.

Valeurs positives

26. **Bienveillance**—Le jeune estime qu'il est très important d'aider les autres.
27. **Égalité et justice sociale**—Le jeune accorde beaucoup d'attention à la promotion de l'égalité, et à la réduction de la faim et de la pauvreté.
28. **Intégrité**—Le jeune agit selon ses convictions et défend ses croyances.
29. **Honnêteté**—Le jeune « dit la vérité même si ce n'est pas facile ».
30. **Responsabilité**—Le jeune accepte et assume ses propres responsabilités.
31. **Abstinence**—Le jeune croit qu'il est important d'éviter d'être sexuellement actif et de consommer de l'alcool ou d'autres drogues.

Compétences sociales

32. **Planification et prise de décisions**—Le jeune sait comment planifier à l'avance et faire des choix.
33. **Aptitudes interpersonnelles**—Le jeune fait preuve d'empathie et de sensibilité, et noue des amitiés.
34. **Aptitudes culturelles**—Le jeune connaît des personnes d'autres cultures, races et ethnies, et se sent à l'aise avec elles.
35. **Résistance**—Le jeune est capable de résister à des pressions négatives exercées par ses pairs et à des situations dangereuses.
36. **Résolution pacifique de conflits**—Le jeune tente de résoudre les conflits sans recourir à la violence.

Identité positive

37. **Pouvoir personnel**—Le jeune sent qu'il a le contrôle sur les choses qui lui arrivent.
38. **Estime de soi**—Le jeune affirme avoir un degré élevé d'estime de soi.
39. **Sentiment d'utilité**—Le jeune croit que sa vie a un sens.
40. **Vision positive de l'avenir**—Le jeune est optimiste quant à son avenir personnel.

▶ *I Have a Recipe!* ◀

Please print or type everything so that it is easy to read. Send to Recipes, c/o Publishing, Search Institute, 125 1st Avenue Northeast, Suite 125, Minneapolis, Minnesota 55413. Or fax to 612-376-8956.

Chef (name) _____

Address _____

_____

Phone _____ Fax _____ E-mail _____

School or organization _____

Name of recipe (activity) _____

Nutrients (developmental assets) _____

Serves (number and age of primary recipients) _____

Ingredients (materials, equipment, coordination, other resources) _____

_____

_____

_____

Instructions (use extra pages if necessary):

1. _____

_____

_____

2. _____

_____

_____

3. _____

_____

_____

4. _____

_____

_____

5. _____

_____

_____

6. _____

_____

_____